ART

Money

SUCCESS

FINALLY MAKE A LIVING DOING WHAT YOU LOVE

A complete and easy-to-follow system for the artist who wasn't born with a business mind. Learn how to find buyers, get paid fairly, negotiate nicely, deal with copycats and **sell more art.**

MARIA BROPHY

Printed in the United States of America

First Printing, 2017

ISBN 10:   978-0-9990115-0-8

Publisher: Son of the Sea, Inc.

10 9 8 7 6 5 4 3 2 1

Dedication

To my mother, the first artist I ever met. She taught me that I could do anything I wanted to do, as long as I put my mind to it. For that, I'm grateful.

And to my soul-mate, Drew, who has believed in me forever. He showed me that you can create your life as you would a painting. Imagine it first, and then allow it to be.

Contents

Introduction

"Success Loves Speed"

—Gary Ryan Blair

Get ready to do everything differently. This book is going to force you to see the art business in a way that no one else ever talks about. It's going to inspire you to sit down and think, in a way that you have never done before. And it's going to bring out answers from deep inside that you didn't know were there.

One of the reasons my husband Drew and I have had success in the art business is because we rarely do things the way artists have been taught. We don't focus on getting Drew's art into galleries, we've never applied for a grant and we have never entered an art contest.

Instead, we've invested time into hard-core thinking and strategizing and we have carved out a unique way to sell art. We have done things in a way that many traditional art snobs would snub us for. But secretly, they dream of having the lifestyle that we live.

WHO THIS BOOK IS FOR

I wrote this book for the artist who wants to learn new strategies to take their art business to the next level, and *is willing to implement them*. This book is for the artist who wants to earn a good living making and selling their art.

Throughout the book I use many real-life examples, most of which have come from my own experiences. You'll notice that many examples are of artists who paint. But please note that the strategies shared could easily apply to any type of artist, medium and style.

This book will be useful for artists who create graphic design, cartoons, paintings, sculptures, photography, watercolor, chalk, murals, illustrations, jewelry and just about anything else.

I wrote this book to help artists learn how to increase their income and make money from their talents. If you are interested in generating more money and success from your art, then this book is for you!

PS... This book is *not* for artists who want to continue working within the old, outdated system of selling art, or for those who feel that art and money don't mix.

SUCCESS LOVES SPEED!

Do you ever wonder why some artists are wildly successful, while others just barely squeak by? And have you noticed that sometimes, talent seems to have very little to do with success?

There are specific strategies that successful artists follow, but most won't talk about them. It may seem like an unfathomable mystery, how some artists are selling their work in high volume while other, more talented artists, are struggling.

I have dedicated the last 20 years of my life towards solving this mystery, by researching the strategies of successful artists and learning how to apply them.

I've found that implementing even just one new strategy can get huge results. Imagine the impact in sales you'll see when you implement new strategy after new strategy, year after year.

Many artists take the time to learn the basics of what they need to do, but very few actually APPLY what they learn. And when you don't apply new knowledge, you don't get the results.

That's why I designed this book to be an *active workbook*; that will encourage you to take action, so you can start seeing results quickly.

As you work through each chapter, you will be guided to take time to THINK, STRATEGIZE and APPLY as you go. If you take the time to implement the strategies in this book, I guarantee you will see results. (And when you do, please email me at consulting@mariabrophy.com so we can celebrate together!)

Throughout the book, I share real life stories about my own experiences, as well as those of other artists that I have helped over the years. Please note that in some of the stories, I have changed personal details to protect their privacy.

Each chapter contains a number of success strategies that will help you level-up your art business and increase your income. Many of the chapters also contain a worksheet of exercises, which is where the true magic of this book lies. When you complete the worksheets as they are presented, you will gain immediate insights you can apply right away.

One of the strategies that all successful people use is SPEED. When a successful person gets an idea, they jump to action quickly. Just sitting around and thinking about something gets you nowhere. When an opportunity or idea arises, you have to take action immediately to get results. Good ideas and opportunities fizzle out and die if you don't act.

Remember: *success loves speed*. The quicker you implement the strategies you learn in this book, the greater the results you will witness... and the faster your art business will grow.

HOW TO USE THIS WORKBOOK - TAKING TIME TO THINK

If you are serious about growing your art business, follow these instructions to the letter. Get yourself a fresh new notebook to write in and a pen that feels great in your hand.

Carve out consistent time every day to work on just one chapter. Every morning (or evening, if that works best for you), choose a time when you can be alone and undisturbed for at least an hour.

Have pen and paper in hand. Read one chapter and take time to sit and think about how it applies to you and what you want. Give yourself up to an hour to THINK each day.

If there's a worksheet with the day's chapter, work on that. If there isn't, use your notebook to take notes and ask yourself how the information can be applied to your situation.

If you don't know all the answers to the worksheet questions, don't worry. Just do your best to come up with any answer, even if it's not perfect. Over time, I promise, answers will come.

This process of "taking time to think" is one that is only practiced by the truly successful. When we take time to purposefully THINK each day, we uncover solutions that we didn't know were there. And from these realizations, we will make corrections to our business practices and ultimately get results.

This book is designed to be revisited many times over the course of your career. As time goes by, your desires and needs will evolve. I recommend that you go through this workbook every year and do the exercises all over again, with an evolved perspective, as you fine-tune your art business.

Before you even proceed to the rest of this book, take a minute to think about what you want out of life and how you envision your career as an artist. Write these things down in your notebook. Then continue to the next chapter. Yes, I'm asking you to think before you sit down to think!

I'm glad you picked up this book, because it's my life mission to help artists create the lifestyle and business they dream of. If this book helps you to get there, then my life mission is complete!

1

HOW I MASTERED THE BUSINESS OF ART

The insurance industry was my bread and butter, until I met an artist named Drew Brophy. It was 1996, and he was only twenty-five years old. His lifestyle was fascinating; he was painting surf art for a living while traveling to surf spots all over the world. I remember watching this long haired surfer paint surfboards while sitting on the floor of his San Clemente beach apartment. Right away, I saw immense potential in his work and I felt compelled to be a part of it.

While working my full time job at the insurance company, I helped Drew part time. I started by handling his marketing. I was able to get him many media interviews, which helped with sales of his work. Then I developed a program where we sold his art prints to surf shops. All of this was done on the weekends and evenings, as I had a 9-5 job to go to every day.

We got married, and a few years later Drew finally convinced me to quit my corporate job to work with him full time. Friends said that it was nuts for me to leave that nice salary, but I did it. And our son was just three years old at the time.

I'll admit it, I was afraid to give up my security, benefits and 401K program. But the lure of a life of adventure and doing what I loved was stronger than my practical concerns.

I called my friend Lauren and asked for advice. She had previously left a high paying job to live her dream of being a writer. She told me what I needed to hear: "Once you leave that job, your new life will begin and you'll never look back." And she was right.

The day I left that corporate job was the day my life truly began. I was free to create my own business, to travel when I wanted, and to be there for my kids. And the best part was that I was doing what I loved.

However, once I'd left my job, I realized that the art business was tougher than I'd imagined. I had to figure out how to increase Drew's art sales to cover the income that we'd just lost. I had NO IDEA how to take our sales to a higher level.

It wasn't enough that Drew was talented. I quickly learned that there was much more to financial success in art than talent. It became my quest to learn the ins and outs of making a living as an artist. We created a rough business plan and strategy and we figured the rest out as we went.

As I dug deeper into learning about art sales, I was shocked to find that many artists who were winning prestigious awards and had a big name in the traditional fine art world weren't even able to support their families with their art.

I was introduced to one very well-known artist who sells her art in fine New York galleries and has won numerous awards. She was a big deal in her town. I was excited to learn more about her path, until it was revealed to me that she worked as a full time secretary and that her art was not supporting her.

It became clear to me that awards and accolades alone weren't the path to a financially successful art business. Then I found other artists who were virtually unknown in the fine art world, but were literally earning hundreds of thousands a year in art sales! I thought to myself "how can this be?"

There are games being played all around us. There is the game of the poor artist paradigm, the game of the artist seeking to win accolades and then there is the game of the financially successful artist. I discovered that you can choose which game you want to play. I decided to learn the game of the financially successful artist. I continued to study these artists to learn their secrets.

The financially successful artists were not applying for grants or entering contests. Instead, they were employing the strategies of business owners and putting an artistic spin on it.

As I learned one new strategy after another, we began to see an increase in Drew's art sales. We fine-tuned our pricing and marketing and we made deals with larger companies that helped us take his art to the mainstream market.

We started adding multiple streams of income into the mix. We learned about art licensing and how to generate money over and over again from one single painting.

Drew's name became synonymous with surfing and art in the world of action sports. He began getting larger and larger opportunities from companies, licensees and art collectors.

We stopped doing business with time-wasters and energy suckers. We put an end to giving art away and learned how to generate huge profits just by making a few small changes in the way we worked with clients.

It wasn't always easy. We learned hard lessons, had some great successes and quite a few failures. Our tenacity resulted in being able to support our family of four, in a Southern California beach town, with the income generated from a mere surf artist.

Multiple streams of income and being open to learning new strategies is what keeps us in business, even when the economy is bad. We have consistently earned well over six figures every three to six months since 2001.

The irony is this: Neither Drew nor I have had formal art training. Drew had only one art class in college and then he decided to go right to work as an artist after high school. Instead of academic training, Drew and I have spent many years discovering, testing and applying the strategies of truly successful artists. And now I am passing this information onto you.

2

DECIDE WHAT YOU WANT

Your life is a series of days, leading into months and then into years. How you spend your days is literally what your entire life will look like.

Think about that for a moment. **What you do every day defines your life.** Imagine that it's a decade into the future, and you are looking at the last ten years of your life. What kind of life have you lived? Is this what you wanted? If the answer is yes, then you are on the right track. If the answer is no, then it's time to make a change.

So we need to begin this journey by getting to know what you really want, so you can set the right kind of goals—the kind that will motivate you to take action. To get started, all I want you to do right now is answer this question:

How do you want your daily life to look?

Your answer will determine everything you do from this point forward. What you choose to do with your time every day is what your life becomes. If you are focusing on doing the things you love on most days, you will have a life without regrets.

The problem is that life can get complicated. There are many demands tugging on us every day, begging for our attention. Our minds are so scattered that we don't always take the time to figure out what it is that we want for ourselves, or to recognize that *this isn't it*.

It is said that people spend more time planning their vacations than they do planning their lives. This is sad, because if we don't take the time to plan out what we want for ourselves, we will end up living a life someone else wanted for us.

There's a great book called *The Top Five Regrets of the Dying*, written by a caretaker who nursed terminal patients. The author wrote that the number one regret of the dying was this:

"I wish I'd had the courage to live a life true to myself, not the life others expected of me."

Too many people are not living the life they want to live. Every week, month and year that goes by without living out your passions, the farther away they get from you.

The death of a dream happens silently and slowly. When you're young, you go along with what everyone else is doing and what they expect of you. You fail to take the time to get clarity on what you want. You shove your dreams to the side, as people convince you that they aren't important. Decades fly by, as you're too busy taking care of everything else, instead of building the life you really want. One day you wake up, old and tired, and realize you've done everything "right"—except you forgot to do the things that you had dreamed of as a kid.

I don't want this to happen to you. I don't want you to have any regrets, or feel frustrated that your art career never took off the way you'd hoped. But I'm confident that it won't, because if you are the type of person to read books like this, then you are probably a person who takes control of your life (or if you haven't been in the past, maybe you're ready to now).

No matter what your age, whether you're a budding artist or one with decades of experience, today you will get greater clarity and make a plan to design the life and business you want.

GETTING CLARITY

The first time I really understood the importance of getting clarity on what you really want was back in 1996. Drew and I had only been dating for about a month at the time. I was in his room, and something on top of his desk caught my eye.

It was a piece of paper, neatly typed up, and the title at the top read "MY LIFE by DREW BROPHY".

The paper was separated into five paragraphs, each one representing a segment of his life and a description of what he envisioned.

He had written under the ART section that he wanted to become the best known surfboard artist in the world. Under the SURFING section he wrote that he wanted to surf the world's best big wave spots, including those in places like Tahiti, Peru and Indonesia.

The paragraph that caught my eye was the one titled FAMILY. He described in detail his desired life of traveling the world with his wife and kids, while surfing and making art.

It was astounding to me that a 25 year old surfer had this much clarity on what he wanted. He had mapped out his entire life on one little piece of paper.

When I read the words, I felt a great excitement stirring inside me. I knew that this was a life I could see myself living, as I had also dreamed of it as a child. Yet, until that moment, I didn't know it was possible.

Not once in high school did any teacher tell me that a business of traveling and art was a possible career choice. If I would have told a counselor at college that this was my plan, they would have advised me to find a real job.

That very day, in 1996, I decided that I, too, would create a life of travel and adventure, and find a way to be paid while doing it. Ever since then, I have made sure that every decision I made brought me closer to that reality.

Now, twenty years later, everything that Drew wrote on that piece of paper has come true.

YOUR ART IS YOUR LIFE

There's a plethora of art critics, consultants and gallery owners that will tell you how to run your art business. There are set ways of doing things in the art world, and if you are the maverick that decides to do something different, you may be criticized. There are rules and guidelines and opinions, all meant to control how artists behave.

Don't follow any of these rules and guidelines. Not unless they fit with your plan. I don't want you to follow my advice, either, not unless it resonates with you. You are the one who has to live with your decisions. So make sure that your decisions are yours, not someone else's.

As a successful creative, your art becomes your life. Your work life and your personal life spills into and over each other. Your art becomes intertwined with how you spend your days, the people you surround yourself with and the places you go.

This is why it is crucial for an artist to be the sole director of their art, career and lifestyle. No one else can decide for you. It's important for *you* to decide where you want to go, and then implement the strategies in this book to help you get there.

WHAT DOES SUCCESS LOOK LIKE TO YOU?

Success has a different meaning for each person. Most of the artists I work with say that they will consider themselves successful once they can support their family with their art.

Some will only consider themselves successful when they have reached a desired achievement or have impacted the world in a positive way with their art.

Only you can decide what success means to you. Below are examples of what success looks like to some people:

- Earning a healthy income to support a family

- Living a lifestyle that enables you to do the things you love
- Developing a reputation for creating meaningful art
- Making a true difference in the world with art
- Developing a technique that becomes a new standard in the art world
- Becoming known as the best in your genre

You need to find your own definition of success, one that feels right for you. On the next page is the Artist Clarity Worksheet, which will guide you to determining what you really want.

IMPORTANT: To get the most out of all of the exercises in this book, don't type your answers into a computer or electronic device. Instead, write your answers into a notebook or in this book. Using pen on paper accesses a part of your brain that is wired to find answers that are deep inside you. This is what will help you get results. If this doesn't make sense to you, do it anyway. Often, we don't even know the answers we are seeking, but when we sit and quietly write on paper, ideas and thoughts come to us.

If you don't know what to write, then write anything you want, just to get the energy flowing. The process of writing leads your mind to grasp for answers, often buried deep inside you. Take your time daydreaming as you answer the questions. Make sure to enjoy the process—dreaming about your ideal lifestyle should be fun and fill you with enthusiasm (if it doesn't, keep exploring until you find a vision that does!)

ARTIST CLARITY WORKSHEET

Date_____ Instructions: Every 6 months, complete this form and review your previous sheets. Your answers will change as you grow.

What does overall success look like to me? How will I know when I've become successful?

(Be specific – if money means success to you, how much do you have to earn a year to feel successful? If it's a set of achievements, specify what they are.)

What do I want to spend my time doing, on most days? What is the ideal lifestyle for me?

What is the one thing that I could accomplish that would take my art business to the next level?

What is my number one, most important goal for my art business this year?

What do I intend to become <u>known for</u> in ten years?

What new skills do I intend to learn that will further my art business?

How much money do I intend to earn?

Yearly $_____ Monthly $_____ Weekly $_____

NAME of two influential people that I wish to meet this year:

_____

NOW THAT YOU KNOW WHAT YOU WANT

When we write things down, they become clear in our sub-conscious minds. This is where the magic occurs, because from this point forward, your mind will immediately recognize opportunities that will bring you closer to your goals.

Once you can recognize such opportunities, you will be likely to take action on them, which will lead straight to the goals you've written down.

When you are clear on what you want, your mind will also start generating powerful ideas, usually at the most random times (when in the shower or taking a walk). Acting on these "eureka" ideas will quickly bring your goals to you.

WHAT IF YOU DON'T KNOW WHAT YOU WANT?

Some people tell me they aren't sure what they want from their lives. But when I press them to dig deep into their childhood dreams, they discover that they really knew all along. Their desires had just gotten buried underneath everyone else's plans for them.

If you are struggling with deciding what you want, go easy on yourself. Take time to think. Go someplace quiet and clear your mind.

Think back to a time when you were young and dreaming of your future. What did you imagine? What did you dream of? Often we find clues that go way back to when we were children.

Sometimes we don't know what we want because our desires have been marginalized or suppressed, due to the negative influences from people in our past. This is common for those who have had controlling people in their lives or circumstances that have held them back from taking care of themselves.

Do the exercise anyway. Even if you have no idea what to write, sometimes just by sitting down and grabbing a pen, you'll get a clearer idea of what you want. Once you start writing with the intention and give yourself permission to explore your desires, you may find that they flow out magically onto the paper.

One extra exercise that will help if you're stuck: Take a blank sheet of paper and write at the top of it: "What do I want?" Start writing a list of anything and everything, including the small and silly. This exercise will unleash your subconscious mind. You might be surprised at how many words and ideas you end up writing down.

Once you've written down a clear, defined list of what you want, it is now able to manifest.

Keep the list or the Artist Clarity Worksheet that you wrote and read it daily. This will help you stay on track and remind you of what is most important to you, so that you don't get sidetracked. When we stay on track, we achieve what we plan to achieve. Every six months, or sooner if you feel necessary, re-visit your list and update it as you reach your goals. Then replace them with new ones.

Never throw these worksheets away. Years from now you will read them and be surprised at how many of the things you wrote down came to fruition.

3

HOW TO BEGIN

"The secret to making a living as an artist is that there are no secrets. Artists find their own paths, and each path is unique."

—Alyson Stanfield,
author of *I'd Rather be in the Studio*

Where does one BEGIN with their art career? It seems as though there aren't any clearly defined road maps for the art business.

There are lots of books on the market that teach artists how to get grants and residencies and how to enter art contests. But none of these things fit into a long term business plan. You can't support a spouse and three kids off of contest winnings!

An artist emailed me recently and asked, "I'm creating art but not selling it yet. Where do I start?" There is no one way to create an art career. There are many different variables that determine the best plan for you, such as the type of art you create, the theme, your personality, your desired outcome, etc. There are literally thousands of different paths you can take, and the best one for you will reveal itself as you begin to take action.

The first step is to commit to becoming a master at your craft and creating art that will be of great value to your buyers. Then commit to building a strong foundation for your art business. You create a strong foundation when you:

1. Know what you want and plan in congruence with that (every decision you make should be with "what you want" in mind)
2. Determine your niche and who your right buyer is (a.k.a. Target Market)
3. Generate a powerful plan to connect with your right buyer and to get the sales and lifestyle you want
4. Operate your Art Business like a business

The following chapters will help you work through the steps shown above. You don't have to get it all figured out perfectly right now—your goals and dreams will evolve as time goes on.

BRAINSTORM HOW TO REACH YOUR IDEAL CLIENT/COLLECTOR

Every breakthrough I've ever had began with a brainstorming session. There is not one book or course on the market that can do your thinking for you. You have to do it yourself.

The reason you can't find resources to do your thinking for you is because when it comes to art, the answers vary depending on the artist, the type of art, the price points, the fans, location and a hundred other factors.

The exercise below will help your mind access solutions that are right for you. Grab a pen and your notebook, give yourself ten minutes to think, and answer the following questions:

1. Describe your ideal client or collector. (i.e. people who love horses and live in the countryside who earn over $100,000/year)
2. Where can you find these people? What clubs do they join, where do they go for pleasure, where do they live or work? (i.e. at equestrian events/races)
3. What is one action that you can take today to connect with your ideal client or collector? (i.e. make a phone call, join a club, sign up to be on a newsletter list, ask for an introduction, offer to exhibit at one of their events, etc.)

Below are some examples of specific types of artists, and possible action plans to reach collectors who may be interested in their work. Keep in mind, these examples are simplified and are being shown to illustrate a general path an artist can take.

Contemporary Artist: You are a fine artist and your goal is to sell your contemporary paintings to high profile collectors. First, create art that will be of value to your target market. This requires you to refine your skills and master your craft. Next, determine the best way to reach those high profile collectors. It could be via galleries that cater to your target market, or through art consultants or by using an entirely new strategy.

Then take steps to become eligible to get into those galleries or to connect with those consultants.

Illustrator: Your goal is to illustrate artwork for the campaigns of Fortune 500 companies. First, generate a portfolio with a few examples of your work that shows your ability. Next, obtain a list of advertising agencies and marketing agencies that work directly with Fortune 500 companies. Then set up meetings to give presentations of your work to those agencies.

Photographer: Your goal is to explore the world and become globally known as the photographer of nearly extinct wildlife, bringing global attention to help save the species. Work on becoming a master at your craft. Connect with organizations who are helping to save nearly extinct species. Next, find a way to work with them, providing your services and contributing to their cause. Find out what you need to do to get hired or raise money to send you to remote areas of the world so you can do the work you want to do.

Pop Artist: Your goal is to become one of the world's best selling pop artists. First, you would work to build up a collector base through exhibits, online sales and retail or gallery sales. You would devise several different channels to sell high volume art print reproductions. You would develop a newsletter list to keep in constant contact with your collectors and retailers. You would devise strategies to create a frenzied demand for your reproductions.

Surfboard Artist: (This was Drew's path). Your goal is to become the world's best known surfboard artist. Refine your skills. Develop a technique and style that will make your work memorable. Next, seek out jobs painting at surfboard factories for the best shapers and surfers in the world. Insist on signing your name to every surfboard you paint. Paint thousands of surfboards over the course of a decade.

Drew followed this plan of action consistently for many years. With time and focused energy, he honed his painting skills and got so good and fast that he was painting up to ten surfboards a day. He became well-known for his surfboard art and companies sent him all over the world to paint. Now, twenty years later, he can say that he has reached his goal.

Use these examples to create your own general art career plan. The following chapters will help you get to the fine details.

4

ESTABLISH A NICHE

"It's okay to do a lot of different things.
But if you want to sell your work,
you have to focus on just one market at a time."
—Maria Brophy

Establishing a "niche" means to place your focus into one specialty area, creating a specific style or type of work and marketing it to a specific buyer.

When selling art, it's easier to make sales within a small niche than it is to sell to the impossibly large niche of "everyone."

Take, for example, an artist who only paints equestrian themed art. Selling art that depicts horses is much easier than selling a general theme. This is because it's easier to find buyers of horse art; you simply reach your buyers by going to equestrian themed events, races and charities. You are guaranteed that almost everyone at an equestrian event loves horses.

Mary Engelbreit is one of the top-selling illustrators in the world. She reached success over thirty years ago when she developed a popular greeting card line. Later, she went on to license her art for thousands of products. Her colorful illustrations target the niche of women, specifically mothers. Her work is sold on products that mothers buy and in stores where mothers shop. Her illustrations and captions perfectly appeal to her target audience.

It's much easier to reach a target audience when you work within a clearly defined niche. And then, when you reach that target audience, you can use the right language to speak directly to them and entice them to buy.

In the case of Mary Engelbreit, she wouldn't sell her products in men's stores, nor would she market to teenage girls. She is laser focused on her target market, and all of her marketing language and advertising is designed to reach and attract her target niche market.

That's why this is so effective; when you design your art marketing to attract a niche market, you are speaking directly to them, using language that resonates with them. And when you speak directly to them, they will better connect with your work and want to buy.

Having an established niche gets results in just about any business. When I started writing my blog, I wrote specifically for artists about the business of art.

One of my friends warned me, "If you want your blog to be popular, stop writing for artists. Write for a wider audience."

He meant well, but he was wrong. I discovered that when I wrote specifically about the business of art, I would get a greater response from readers.

Once I figured this out, I decided to follow my passion and write just for artists. After all, that's where my knowledge and experience is. Writing for a small niche has gained me more readers, not less.

When I tell artists that they, too, will have greater success if they market within a niche, many tell me that they struggle to figure out what their niche is.

Some artists say they don't want a niche, because they like creating in a variety of themes and mediums and markets. They don't want to feel constricted.

If this is you, know this: It's okay to work on a variety of themes and mediums. Never stop experimenting with a lot of different things.

But if you want to sell your work in high volume, you have to choose a niche to focus on when marketing your art. Focus is necessary if you want to make a living selling your work.

You'll have a tough time creating financial success by trying to be known as "the artist who does everything."

If you are one who is resisting selling within a niche, don't give up on this strategy just yet. Read on, and maybe we can help you carve out a niche that feels good to you.

HOW A NICHE HELPS YOUR WORK STAND OUT

Below are commonly asked questions that I receive from artists:

- How do I stand out in a field that is so competitive?
- How do I find people who will love my work?
- How do I get my paintings in front of more buyers?

The answer to all of these questions is the same; and that is, to establish a niche. When we focus in one area, and we consistently work on it, we get better and better at it. Eventually, we become the go-to person in that niche. We become KNOWN for our work. Once we are known for it, people will *come to us* for it. See how that works?

Think of some of the most famous artists and you'll see they all worked within a niche. I'll give you a few examples that come to my mind:

- Anne Geddes: photographer of tiny babies placed in flowers and plants
- Thomas Kinkaide: painter of little cottages in bucolic settings
- Jackson Pollock: used a unique technique of "splatter and action" pouring paint on canvas
- Keith Haring: a distinctive style of pop art with theme of New York culture

Many artists start by experimenting with lots of styles, until they find something they're good at that people love. Then they stop experimenting and double down on that style, making it their own.

We can also look at many not-quite-as-famous artists who have found their niche and are incredibly successful. The examples below are all living artists who have built up profitable businesses and are making a good living with their art. I recommend you look them up online and see what they are doing:

- Clark Little: photographs the shore-break of waves in Hawaii
- Wyland: paints whales and sea life
- Michael Goddard: paints playful olive characters in martini glasses
- Fabio Napoleoni: paints the theme of sad characters and hearts

The best example I can share is the one in which I have direct experience, and that's with marketing Drew's work in the super micro-niche of surf art.

Drew started his art career painting surfboards. I don't know of a smaller niche than that. Surfing is only enjoyed in coastal areas where there are waves. And, of the few surfers out there, a small percentage can afford to buy art, and of those, only a fraction are buyers of Drew's art.

But, the benefit of being an artist in a small niche was this: his name became well-known as the artist who painted surfboards. After twenty-five years of being known for surf art (and teaching thousands of artists his techniques), Drew is one of the most sought after surfboard artists alive today. His fine art surfboards are some of the highest priced on the market and are collected by celebrity musicians and athletes.

Had Drew attempted to become known for painting "anything and everything," his career would have gone a little differently. Being known as a surf artist has not stopped Drew from experimenting with other themes and mediums. Painting surfboards is now only a small part of what he does. His newer passion is working within another small niche; sacred geometry art.

For each niche, we focus our marketing and sales directly to the buyer. For Drew's sacred geometry art, we directly target people who have an interest in quantum physics, mathematics and the metaphysical. For Drew's surf art, we target people who love the ocean and surfing lifestyle.

Here's another example of marketing directly to your niche rather than marketing your art broadly. In 2015 we invested monthly in advertising Drew's sacred geometry fine art in a beautiful Laguna Beach art magazine which was widely distributed. We were disappointed that after a year, we still hadn't received any calls from the ad. It was an expensive investment that got zero results.

We moved our advertising to a much smaller magazine that catered to people interested in the metaphysical. Within two days of the magazine hitting the stands, we received two phone calls that led to new collectors of Drew's sacred geometry art!

The success of the ad was due to the fact that our advertisement spoke directly to the readers; it focused on the meditation features of the art. Marketing directly to people, within a niche, and positioning it to appeal to their passions and interests, will be more successful than targeting everyone and hoping someone likes it.

NICHE CATEGORIES

Establishing a niche doesn't mean that you can't experiment with new themes or styles. It just means that you will choose one area to focus your marketing efforts on, so that you experience greater results in sales.

If you are working in different styles and themes, choose your most popular or favorite to focus on marketing first. After focusing on that for a few years, and growing sales and a reputation for it, then you can branch out and market in another niche as well.

If you're still unsure how to establish a niche, here are a few examples:

1. **Style:** If you have a very distinctive style, or medium that you use, or technique that you invented, this could be your "niche."

   A great example of a niche style is my good friend, photographer Matt Schwartz, who is known for creating large format Polaroids of girls, surfing and global travels. He has a very distinct style; his work is so distinct, that when others attempt to mimic his style, it's evident.

2. **Lifestyle:** This is the easiest niche to establish. If you are passionate about a particular lifestyle, hobby, sport or activity, your passion can be your niche.

   For example, artist Guy Harvey. He's an avid fisherman and diver, and he paints fish and ocean lifestyle related images. He is extremely well-known for his fishing lifestyle art.

   Below are a few more examples of lifestyles that can be established as your niche:

   - Harley Biker
   - Bird Watcher
   - Adventure sport

- African (or insert location here) Travel photographer
- Gamer
- Gardening
- Cooking
- Theater

3. **Geographic Location:** Become known as the artist of your local community. This works very well in tourist areas.

   The small beach town that I live in, San Clemente, CA, has an artist that has been known as the "local San Clemente artist" for decades. All of Paul Gavin's paintings are of the San Clemente lifestyle, which includes landscapes and beach lifestyle scenes. His art is displayed in the local post office and the City of San Clemente has commissioned him to create art for outdoor installations all over town.

   A brilliant move he made many years ago was to team up with a busy, local restaurant on the San Clemente pier. On weekends, he's outside on the patio of the restaurant, exhibiting and selling his work to tourists and locals. He does very well being known as the San Clemente artist.

4. **Purpose:** Become known as the artist who is for or against something or who is helping to raise awareness of a cause or a need by society.

   Artist Kate Sikorski dedicated her time to creating a surf camp for Muslim women. She called it the Burkini Project, which allowed Muslim women to enjoy the ocean, utilizing swimsuit technology that preserved their religious values while allowing them to surf. Kate then created a series of large-scale mixed media drawings that documented the event in art.

YOUR NICHE

Now, let's figure out what your niche is. The Establish Your Niche Worksheet on the next page will help you. It's time to go deep and think.

Thinking is our greatest tool. When we allow ourselves time to think every day and write down our questions and brainstorm solutions, we will lay out a foundation for our career that will be strong and successful.

Right now, while this chapter is fresh in your mind, grab a pen and go sit somewhere quiet. Be prepared to take time and truly reflect and consider the answers you write on the worksheet.

ESTABLISH YOUR NICHE WORKSHEET

Name:_____Date_____

Instructions: Answer the questions below. Don't worry if you don't have all the answers right away. They will come.

What hobbies or activities do I love doing the most? (Lifestyle)

Where would I be happiest living? (Location i.e. beach, mountains, Paris)

What do I really feel passionate about? (People, places, things)

What is one thing that sets my work apart from others? (Style, medium, theme, etc.)

What project did I do in the past that I really, really enjoyed, and that flowed out of me easily?

Why was it so easy for me? (The people, medium, project, or what?)

Where do I WANT to focus my time and efforts? (Not "should" but "want")

Based on the answers above, what aspects stand out?

EXAMPLE: If you wrote that you love painting island flowers with oils and you live on Maui and you're so passionate about flowers that the work just flows out of you, your niche would be that of a "<u>Maui artist who creates oil paintings of local island flowers</u>."

5

TELL STORIES

While at a dinner party at my friend Steve's house I asked about the art above his living room couch. It was a painting of a little boy playing with a red toy airplane. Steve was excited that I asked and he proudly retold the story the artist had given him about what inspired him to paint the boy and the airplane.

When we have an art exhibit, much of my time is spent telling people the stories behind each piece of art. I'll point to Drew's painting titled TREE OF LIFE and tell about when Drew went on a surf trip to Tahiti and this painting was inspired by a story an old Tahitian woman told him. She explained that the breadfruit trees in Tahiti provided the main food source for Tahitians in times past. This tree was so important to them that generations of families would tend to the family trees with great reverence. She said "when you see a big, old breadfruit tree on someone's property, you know that their grandparents and their grandparent's grandparents tended to that tree, and in turn it gave them life with its fruit."

Every artwork has a story behind it. Tell the story so people can latch onto it and build a personal connection with it. Then they'll be proud to own the piece because the story resonates with them. They will retell the story when it's in their own space.

TELL THE STORY OF YOUR LIFE

Art collectors want to know what inspired you to become an artist and what drives you to continue to create. Every person has a life story. Stories connect us to each other and they evoke emotions and feelings. Our own stories might seem boring to us, because we lived it. But to others, your story will be interesting.

One of my favorite artist stories is that of painter Joshua Paskowitz, who is a friend of mine. He is the youngest of nine siblings who were all raised in a camper van without traditional schooling. His father was a doctor who dropped out of society and took his wife and kids on a twenty-five year adventure, traveling from beach to beach, surfing and living a non-conventional life. Their journey is so intriguing that a movie was made about them called Surfwise.

You can make any life story interesting, even if you grew up in a normal family in a small town where the most exciting thing that ever happened was when Alumni Park got a new children's slide installed. Your story could be told in this way:

"I grew up in Battle Creek, Iowa, population 750. We had to ride a bus over 60 miles to go to school. On some winter days the snow would be so high that our bus driver had to follow close behind the snow plow to get us there. On my fifteenth birthday I got a paint-by-numbers kit as a gift from my Uncle Mac. We had just survived an extra harsh winter, and I was inspired by the redeeming warmth of spring. I decided to paint my own scene instead of the one outlined on the canvas. It was of a field of freshly cut hay, which I could see outside my bedroom window. My parents loved my painting and said that I was an artist. I believed them and at that moment I knew what I wanted to be when I grew up."

Take your story, no matter how boring or exciting you think it is, and find a way to tell it in an interesting way. Include it in your Biography in your portfolio, on your "About" page on your website and repeat it any time someone asks about you. People will remember your story and then they will remember you.

Let's take a break from reading for a moment so you can write out your story. Grab a pen and your notebook and take a little time to think. Answer the following questions:

1. MY STORY: What is one interesting, memorable or unique story I will tell buyers about myself or my life? (i.e. how I became an artist, how I learned to create in the way that I do, etc.)
2. What is one interesting story I can tell about my most current artwork?

6

HOW TO FIND YOUR "RIGHT BUYERS"

"The doors will be opened for those
bold enough to knock."

—Tony Gaskins

At a street fair, I watched as an artist glumly took down her art prints from her booth at the end of the day. Sensing her disappointment, I asked how sales were.

"I didn't sell one darn thing today," she answered sadly.

She was an ocean photographer and her work was absolutely stunning. It was printed on quality canvas art prints and beautifully framed. So what went wrong? Keep reading, I'll get to that in a minute...

If you want to sell more of your work, you have to set the intention to DELIBERATELY CONNECT with the right buyers. Many artists mistakenly attempt to sell to everyone or anyone. They will randomly post their art on social media, exhibit at shows or set up a table at street fairs, without *purposely targeting* their right buyers. Without a well thought out plan to connect with your right buyers, you will just be spinning your wheels.

In this chapter, I'm going to guide you to first determine who your right buyers are. And then we will brainstorm ideas that will connect you with your right buyers. Once you connect with the right buyers, your sales will increase significantly, and you'll write to tell me that this ended up being your best year ever!

WHAT IS A "RIGHT BUYER"?

The "Right Buyer," also known as a "Target Market," is someone who:

- Can connect with the work you do and loves it
- Shares your personal values, lifestyle or passion
- Sees the value of your work
- Is capable of paying your prices

Many artists are trying to sell to the wrong people and then they get frustrated that no one is buying.

A great example of this is the photographer I mentioned earlier. She had everything going for her, so why didn't she sell anything?

She was targeting the wrong people. Her art prints were properly priced over $500, but that venue was not appropriate for sales in that price range. That particular street fair was attended by lower income families who were looking to buy cheaper items priced under $100. The photographer's right buyers were not in that crowd of people.

Her right buyer will be someone who loves the ocean, owns a large home with big wall space, and will have an income of $100,000 or higher.

To sell her art, she will need to go where her right buyers go.

HOW TO FIND YOUR RIGHT BUYERS

Let's go back to the last chapter on Establishing Your Niche. When you have a defined niche, it's much easier to find and connect with your right buyers. (And if you still think you aren't working within a niche, look a little closer. You may already have one, even if you haven't realized it yet.)

As an example, consider Guy Harvey—the artist who lives the lifestyle of fishing and diving. His right buyers are people who fish and dive and who live or love that lifestyle.

Guy Harvey's right buyers live in coastal communities in the South East and Caribbean, shop in fishing and diving shops and they have an income of over $100,000. Many of his right buyers own boats and spend their money on fishing gear, clothing, and artwork that reminds them of the fishing lifestyle.

Guy Harvey is famous in Florida; that's where most of his right buyers live the lifestyle his art is inspired by. He reaches his right buyers through licensing his art for fishing and diving related products that sell to his right buyers through outdoor retailers. He also sells original art and prints.

On the next page is a worksheet that will help you brainstorm where you can find your right buyers. Find a quiet spot, grab a pen, and let's go think.

MY RIGHT BUYER WORKSHEET

Instructions: This is a brainstorming session, so ALL ideas are valid. We want to *get into the head* of your right buyer.

How did past buyers find my art? (i.e. word of mouth, exhibits, Facebook, Etsy, etc.)

What is the income of my right buyer? (i.e. if you're selling art under $500 it might be $50,000. If you're selling art over $5,000, it might be $150,000+).

Where do my right buyers live? (i.e. if you're a "local" artist, they would live in your town. If you are a mountain-themed artist, it would be the mountains, etc.)

Whom does my art appeal to the most? (i.e. Age, gender, lifestyle, income) Ex: If you're creating baseball themed art priced at $500, men between the ages of 35-65 who love baseball and earn $50,000/year) would be your right buyer.

Where do my right buyers spend their spare time? (i.e. traveling to the mountains, black tie events, at sports games, at certain trade shows, etc.)

Write down what kind of art you make and who it will appeal to—and then write a few places your right buyers are likely to hang out or events they will attend.

For example, "I create environmental art that demonstrates the damage caused by plastics in the earth. My right buyers are passionate about saving the world and attend black tie events for charities that specialize in this area."

Now, name three entities you will contact, that are already connected to your right buyers:

    1.
    2.
    3.

RIGHT BUYER WRAP-UP

Now that we have established WHO your right buyer is, HOW MUCH money they make, and WHERE they spend their time, it will be easier to connect with them.

The next step is to brainstorm new ways to reach your right buyers, by going where they go. Once you start focusing on reaching your right buyers where they actually are, you'll begin to see big things happen in your art career. We are going to stretch and think differently about selling art than you've ever considered before. They aren't teaching this stuff in art school and you won't find it in any other book. But it is one of the most effective ways to get your art into the hands of buyers.

What I'm encouraging you to do is to think differently than most artists think. In the next chapter, we dive deep into HOW to connect with your right buyer in non-conventional ways.

7

REACH YOUR AUDIENCE IN NON-CONVENTIONAL WAYS

We are going to fast track your art sales by bypassing traditional means of selling art. We will do this by accessing other entities that share similar themes, values or concerns as you do.

There are charities, companies and organizations that are *already* reaching your right buyers. You can make a quantum leap in your art sales by teaming up with these entities, so they can introduce your art to their own followers. This one idea could quantum leap your art business—right into wild success.

While art galleries and consignment in boutiques can be one way to sell your work, you'll go broke if you focus solely on that business model. There are very few artists that actually make a full time living exhibiting only at galleries, and if you're one of them, keep doing what you're doing.

For the rest of us, the old way of selling art no longer works. The world has changed drastically since 2008. To make more sales, artists have to take marketing into their own hands and get creative about how to reach art buyers.

If you aren't selling enough art, it means that you aren't reaching enough of your right buyers. The current way many artists reach buyers is through social media, advertising, networking and doing live events.

All of these things work, however, there is a much quicker and better way to reach your right buyers, and no one (except me) is talking about it. It requires brainstorming, non-conventional action and an open mind. If you take the time to learn how to do this, you will see your art sales take a quantum leap.

PROVIDING VALUE

Now that you have completed your *reach my right buyers* worksheet and have listed three entities you will contact, let's get you prepared to team up with these entities.

To get one of these entities excited to team up with you, you'll have to provide value to them. That value is exchanged for payment, recognition, the sharing of your links online or the ability to sell your art at their functions.

To be able to provide value, you first have to know what they need. Sometimes it's evident; for example, if their newsletter looks boring and blah, this makes it easy for you to offer to use your artwork to style up their newsletter, in exchange for links to your website.

But, we never want to assume anything. That's why having a conversation with someone at the organization will bring up ideas and needs that you are not aware of.

A few ideas of how to provide value with your art:

- Your art decorates their newsletter or a portion of their website or digital images
- Your art decorates a physical space such as a stage or room at a function
- You donate art to an auction (be sure to share in the proceeds, more on that later)
- You team up to co-create a marketing campaign or charity event
- Your art goes on printed products that they give out at a function
- Do a live painting, poster signing or performance at a trade show or event

Sometimes it's not evident what a company might need, and so you have to call and ask. But first, do your research on the company so that you have a clear understanding of their mission and their activities and what is important to them. This will make it easier to call and talk to them and connect on a personal level.

Then ask yourself "what value can I bring to them?" Take the time to brainstorm ideas. It could be something as simple as giving them something interesting to offer to their followers.

When you call, have a general plan of what you want to offer and what you want in exchange for that offer. Ask a lot of questions and be flexible if your contact there has a different idea of how you can work together. **Have no expectations and don't be attached to the outcome.** If they aren't interested, thank them for their time and tell them to let you know if they change their mind. Never give up on a potential opportunity. And then move on and call the next person on your list.

Get in the habit of continuously dreaming up non-conventional ways to reach your right buyers. Daily, ask yourself: "What can I do to reach my right buyers? Who can I team up with? Who can I call? Where should I go?"

When we continually ask questions, the answers will come.

EXAMPLES

The most effective and efficient way that Drew and I have reached our right buyers is by teaming up with organizations much larger than ourselves that already deeply connect with large numbers of our right buyers.

Selling art is a numbers game. To sell art in high quantities, you must reach high quantities of people. Only a small percentage of the people who see your work will actually buy, so you have to cast your net wide.

The idea is to reach large numbers of your right buyers at once. This will give you a quantum leap and help you bypass ten years of hard work doing it on your own!

For example: If you are an environmental artist who photographs scenes of nature, your right buyer would be someone who shares the same passion as you for wildlife. They may belong to environmental groups such as The Sierra Club.

Offer to set up an exhibit at an event, allow them to use your art in their newsletters in exchange for a link and mention of you and your website, or license your art for their merchandise. Offer them something of great value in exchange for having access to their members. Set the intention to form a long term relationship with the group for mutual benefit.

Below are a few examples of non-conventional ways to reach your right buyers that I have personally tested:

Team up with a large organization who is already selling to your right buyer (provide something that compliments what they are doing or fills a need for them)

Advertise in the newsletters of charities/organizations that reach your right buyer. The larger their mailing list, the better exposure. You could offer to let them use your artwork to decorate their newsletter, in exchange for a link to your website and a mention of your name.

Exhibit your art at events that cater to your Right Buyer. If there's a large event coming to town, offer to decorate their walls or stage with your art for the evening, in exchange for a booth or the ability to sell your work there and collect emails from attendees.

We offered three of Drew's large art pieces to be displayed on a stage that world famous singer Eddie Vedder and other musicians performed on at a local charity event. All of the ensuing media photos showed Drew's art clearly in the background. This led to new collectors being introduced to his work.

Perform live at trade shows that are in your niche. Trade shows are a very good place to do a live painting, as you are exposed to the decision makers in the industry in which you market to. You can sell your services to do a live painting in the booth of a company exhibiting, or get hired by the event promoter to do a live painting as entertainment for attendees.

Rent a space and curate your own Art Exhibit, and allow a related charity/foundation to set up their own station at the exhibit in exchange for them advertising your exhibit in their newsletter.

Give live painting demonstrations or poster signings at retail stores in your niche (we've done this at surf shops all over the world). Make sure you have something that they can sell of yours during the live event, such as art prints or other products.

Offer use of your art in digital form for Holiday Cards for a niche-related charity/foundation—they will mail it to their large database, and your name and website and art is printed on the front or back of the card.

Put on an exhibit and/or talk at a large event where your right buyers will be present.

License your art to a manufacturer who sells to your right buyers.

Volunteer your time to help at an event that reaches your right buyers. When volunteering, we meet the VIP's and movers and shakers. Offer to decorate the room with your art while you're at it.

All of these ideas require you to aggressively get out of your comfort zone and meet people, but that's what it takes to reach large numbers of potential buyers.

HOW WE REACH DREW'S RIGHT BUYERS AND GET PAID TO DO IT

Over the past twenty years, it took a lot of trial and error, and a lot of brainstorming and bold moves, to figure out what I'm sharing in this chapter. Below are a few of the things we did that worked, in a chronological time-line:

In the 1990's: As an edgy surfboard artist in the late 1990's, Drew's right buyers were males who surf between the ages of 18 and 25 and who loved edgy art.

At the time, we reached Drew's right buyers by teaming up with surfboard manufacturers. Drew would be paid to paint surfboards live at Surf Expo trade shows and other events. While at the events, he reached his right buyers and he connected with companies who sold to his right buyers, which then led to many different licensing deals with those companies.

In the early 2000's: As Drew grew older, his artwork and pricing matured, and his right buyers grew up. After the year 2002, we targeted right buyers aged 25-45, male surfers, with an income of $100,000+ who collected surf style paintings because it reminded them of their passion and youth.

One way that we reached the new right buyers was by teaming up with large organizations with big memberships. For example, we gave Surfrider Foundation digital art for their Christmas Cards one year (which were mailed out to a huge number of right buyers), and we exhibited at black tie events that catered to the right buyers. We also licensed Drew's art for cool products such as skateboards, surfboards and wakeboards. His name was printed on every product, which helped to market his work while being paid for it.

In 2013: Drew's right buyer changed again. He'd moved away from surf art and onto sacred geometry art. His new right buyer is highly educated, wants to change the world, has an understanding of physics and science, and is between 35-65 years old with an income of $250,000+.

To reach Drew's new right buyers, we have to go where they go. One way we have reached the new right buyer was by teaming up with a very large event in Los Angeles called the Conscious Life Expo. Many professionals that teach the concepts that inspire Drew's sacred geometry art are speakers there.

I wanted to reach our new people there, but didn't want to pay for a booth. I wanted to be paid to be there instead, so I found a list of exhibitors that would be at the Expo, and started making phone calls, offering Drew's live painting services in their booths during the event.

The magic of live events is this: you draw people to you when you are creating live. The authors and athletes and mentors that you want to meet will be drawn, like a magnet, to come meet YOU. You become a people magnet when you're performing live.

After a few days of cold-calling and getting nowhere, I finally connected with one exhibitor who said YES! They hired Drew to paint a mural live in their booth during the event.

Over 10,000 people attend the Conscious Life Expo, and I wanted to make an even bigger impact than just having Drew do a live painting in one booth. So I called the promoter of the expo and asked if we could exhibit Drew's new works at the event. It so happened they had a thirty foot wall that was in the main walkway, and the promoter said he would be happy to have Drew hang his art there.

It was a great idea. We exhibited many of Drew's new sacred geometry works on that wall and were able to expose it to over 10,000 people. We were paid to market to our right buyers at a trade show that is attended by some of the most influential people in that field. That one event led to many opportunities and we were able to make a quantum leap with Drew's new style of art.

Since then, the Expo has invited us back year after year, to exhibit on their wall. The consistency of the art hanging on the wall year after year has gained even more leads to sell the art, as attendees remember it and now look forward to seeing the new paintings each year.

One thing you should note about this strategy: Not once was this ever taught in any of the business classes I took. I have not read this strategy in any art business book. But it works! Yet, no one ever does this. But why not?

It's a win-win for everyone. The Expo did us a favor by letting us exhibit the art. But we also did them a favor; we made their thirty foot wall look amazing. It was something that we contributed to them, while gaining promotion for Drew's art. Everyone wins. That's the key to teaming up with others. **Both parties contribute and both parties benefit.** Determining what the benefit might be for the other person, requires you to get on the phone and have a conversation.

Brainstorm ideas. Make a bold move. Get on the phone and call people. That's the magic formula. Let's do a quick exercise right now. Get out your pen and notebook and brainstorm and write the answers to the following:

1. NAME ONE ORGANIZATION or Charity that reaches your right buyer.
2. BRAINSTORM and write down at least three ways that you can team up with them or piggy back on their promotions or events for mutual benefit.

Example: If you paint birds, and your right buyer is a bird watcher, team up with the National Audubon Society. Offer to donate a percentage of sales of your bird paintings in exchange for advertising the paintings in their newsletters (which goes out to over a million bird lovers). Get creative!

They have an "adopt a bird" program, maybe a winner each month gets a print of an artwork of the bird they adopted. Or come up with some other way to make it valuable for the Audubon Society to work with you. Use this example to help get your creative juices flowing! How can you do the same in your own target market?

To gain a stronger understanding of what's important to the organization or charity you named above, sign up to be on their newsletter list. Get familiar with their promotions and what they do, and look for opportunities to team up in the future.

QUICK TIPS ON HOW TO "TEAM UP" WITH AN ORGANIZATION

- Brainstorm ideas on how they will benefit from helping or hiring you (it's not just about you, it's about them too).
- Make phone calls—a lot of them—to the decision makers.
- Don't allow rejections to hurt you. Keep calling people until you find someone interested.
- Offer to provide great value to whomever you team up with up (determine what they will gain from you, such as, you'll make their space look great, you'll provide something special for their customers, etc).
- For every 15 "No's" that you hear, you will get one "Yes"— so don't give up too early.
- Know what you're offering before you make the offer, and be flexible if they want something different.
- Be BOLD and do this! It gets easier as time goes on.

QUANTUM LEAP TO BUYERS WORKSHEET

Name:_____Date_____

Instructions: This is a brainstorming session. Take 15 minutes with a pen to paper and write out 10 ideas for each question. All ideas count!

<u>Who can I team up with, who is already established, to reach my right buyers?</u>

<u>Which large companies would my work be a fit with?</u> (i.e. If you draw robots as your main theme, think tech companies)

<u>Which Large Charities?</u> (i.e. If your art is inspired by a cause or world problem, which charities or celebrities care about the same things?)

<u>Which Trade Shows?</u> (I.e. if your work is music inspired, think NAMM Show or other music industry shows)

<u>Which Events?</u> (i.e. If you paint a horse theme, think equestrian events)

Of the entities and items listed above, name the top three that stand out as viable candidates for a collaboration or mutual arrangement:

1.
2.
3.

Of the three listed above, what can I offer them in exchange for sharing their connections or platform? (Brainstorm many ideas and write them all down)

Three entities that I am committed to contacting this week:

1.
2.
3.

8

THE MINDSET OF SELLING

"Selling is more of a science than a natural born gift."
—Jack White, artist and author of *Magic of Selling Art*.

Most artists hate the act of selling art, but they love having sold it. The mere act of selling art opens us up to the risk of rejection and disappointment. When someone objects to our prices, it is discouraging. When a buyer shows interest but then disappears, we feel frustrated, wondering why.

We were taught that selling art is hard and painful. We learned to fear the rejection when someone says no. We feel weird when discussing money and art in the same conversation.

All of these feelings were learned or passed down through generations of starving artists. But they aren't real or reasonable, and they harm our ability to make money with art.

Thankfully, everything we have learned can be unlearned, by reprogramming our minds with new thoughts, feelings and habits. We can learn to sell art *joyfully*. And when we do, that is one less monkey on our backs. And the art business becomes so much easier.

First, we have to understand that every single thing we do is a habit. Feeling a recurring feeling is also a habit. Feeling uncomfortable selling or discussing money is a habit.

One way to rid yourself of a bad habit is by replacing it with a good one. If you want to quit coffee, you would replace it with herbal tea. If you want to stop hating selling, you can replace that feeling with one of confidence and power.

To make selling easier for you emotionally, you have to develop the habit of separating the personal (my art) from the business (a transaction).

To sell a lot of art, you have to learn the techniques of selling, just like you learned the techniques of creating your art. It took me years to learn how to "sell" and I'm continually working on improving on my sales skills. They get better every day.

There are three things you can do to make selling easy for you:

1. Develop the proper mindset to sell art
2. Allow your clients to spend the money they want
3. Practice, practice, practice techniques of selling until it becomes second nature

BOOST CONFIDENCE WITH POSITIVE THOUGHTS

We have to talk about the mindset first, because your mind is where everything begins. Some artists feel uncomfortable discussing their art and money in the same sentence. They are unsure of their pricing, and worry that they are charging too much or too little. **These worries and feelings come through in the artist's body language and vibrations during a conversation, which makes the buyer feel uncomfortable.** When the buyer feels uncomfortable, they end up not buying.

Here's an example of such a scenario with an artist who is inexperienced at selling: You are showing your work at an event and a potential buyer shows interest. She asks you for a price. You feel weird saying the numbers. You worry it's too much, and so you choke it out in a voice that doesn't sound confident. She feels your weird vibe, and now feels uncomfortable to ask further questions. She changes her mind. She leaves without buying. You think she left because of the price, but you're wrong. She left because of the bad energy you sprinkled on the conversation.

Our thoughts and feelings are energy. Our energy is transferred and is felt very strongly by those we interact with. Think of someone you know that is upbeat and happy. Every time you see this person, you suddenly feel great. This is them transmitting their joyful energy to you. And now think of the person that's always negative and angry. When you see them, you feel icky and drained.

Your thoughts and feelings create an energy that is transmitted directly from you to others. This is why your mindset is so important. If your thoughts are: "I feel weird asking for money. Does this person like my art? Am I any good? What if they don't buy? I'm going to be let down..." you will transmit your uncomfortable feelings out into your voice and your words and even your body language. Your buyer will pick up on those negative feelings and it will kill the sale.

This is a problem that is easily remedied, so if you catch yourself doing this, trust that you can learn how to change your mindset and generate good energy.

Before any event or interaction with a buyer, generate a powerful inner energy of confidence and calm and joy in yourself by doing the following:

1. Prepare in advance by having all of your pricing figured out. Dress in a way that makes you feel confident, and exhibit your art in a way that makes you feel proud.

2. Adopt the belief that your art is a solution to someone else's life. Know that money is an exchange for that solution.

3. Accept that not everyone is going to love your art. Be okay with that.

4. Know that when someone loves your art, they will be happy to pay for it, as it will bring them joy in one way or another. By selling them the art, you are contributing something wonderful to their life.

5. Believe that your art is a contribution to the world. Adopt this belief by repeating it to yourself, over and over again daily.

Say to yourself: "My art is a contribution to the world. People who need my art are happy to exchange money for it. My art is a contribution. My art is a contribution. My art is a contribution."

ALLOW YOUR CLIENTS TO SPEND THE MONEY THEY WANT

If you were raised in a wealthy family where fine artwork was purchased and valued, this section most likely won't apply to you.

But, if you grew up in a lower middle class family, or in poverty, or were raised by parents who had a poor money mindset, you may suffer from an ailment that you aren't even aware you have. And it's this: you have a belief that you are not able to afford things and that there is never enough money. Then you take that belief and you put it on your clients, unknowingly. In doing this, you lower the amount of money your clients will spend on your art. This practice is killing your sales.

Let me explain. And please, give this deep thought, because once you understand this, you will be able to turn it around. When we believe that we can't afford things beyond a certain dollar amount, we subconsciously place our own dollar limits on our clients.

For example, let's say your own personal dollar limit for buying an item for your home is $500. Anything over that and you feel that you just cannot afford it. Now, when a client is looking at the artwork you have available, and you show them one $500 painting and they love it and decide to buy it, you will complete the sale but leave money on the table. In your mind, buying one $500 painting is their limit; because it's *your* limit.

However, once you realize that $500 is your own personal limit, and not theirs, you can offer to sell them a second art piece to compliment the first. And if they say yes to that second piece, you might say, "well, I also have this one over here that would go perfect with the first two that you chose." The truth is, you have no idea how much they might be willing to spend on art. Don't make any assumptions.

This is such a subtle change, but one that has made a huge increase in income for us. When someone walks into our studio and wants to buy one art piece, I then show them a second and a third and so on. I keep offering them more until they say "no, this is enough."

From now on, notice what goes on in your mind when selling. Are you placing your own personal dollar limits on your buyers? With awareness, you can train yourself to stop doing it.

PRACTICE FEELING CONFIDENT

Here are two mind and body techniques to increase your confidence when selling.

Using Body Language: When someone asks how much a piece of your art is, practice feeling confident when you state the price. Let your body language exude confidence, by standing tall, pulling your shoulders back and keeping your arms away from your body.

Open arms means an open heart. Folded arms gives a feeling of being closed off from the person you're talking with. Open your arms away from you so that you give the signal of caring and openness to your buyer. Smile, and confidently discuss what it will take to get this art piece to go home with your buyer and bring them joy.

Over time, this will come easier to you. Just like everything else, discussing art and money is a skill, and if you keep practicing it will become second nature.

Using your mind: Use your conscious mind to direct your thoughts and feelings. If you feel self conscious, focus all of your thoughts on the buyer. Take your mind off of yourself and try to figure out who your buyer really is: what do they love, what do they want and what's important to them? You can do this by asking them questions, such as: "where are you from originally" or "what's your favorite hobby" or "what do you love most about living where you live?"

Don't allow yourself to worry about whether they think your art is good, or what they think of you. When talking to others, you shouldn't be thinking about yourself at all. It distracts you from true connection with the other person. The more we think about ourselves, the more awkward we feel.

If it makes you feel any better, insecurity is common amongst creative people. Many of those who we consider to be great artists have massive feelings of insecurity, even after they have made it big. This is normal and it's okay to feel unsure of yourself sometimes.

Don't allow yourself to feel intimidated by anyone. Your feelings of not being good enough are all in your head. Train yourself to deflect thoughts of being less-than and instead tell yourself "I am enough."

We have the power to reject any thought or feeling that doesn't serve us.

Every time a negative thought pops into your head that says *I'm not good enough* or *who do I think I am to do this great thing*, scream back "I reject that thought." When you tell a thought that you reject it, it goes away. It will come back, but keep rejecting it. After it's been rejected enough times, it will stop coming.

In social situations, when we think too much about ourselves, we feel self-conscious and uncomfortable. It's not possible to think about yourself and about someone else at the same time, so place your mindful focus on your buyer. When you do, your energy will come through as a person who cares, listens and understands.

Your buyers are people. People want to be loved and to feel important. People like people who make them feel loved and important. People buy art from people they like!

And lastly, don't be attached to the need to sell to that person. Feeling desperate to sell puts out a vibration of desperation, which can kill the sale and stress you out while doing it.

Relax. Enjoy the person you're talking to. Encourage the sale, make it easy for them to buy, but don't feel like your day will be ruined if you can't sell it. Be okay with what happens. Allow the outcome to be what it will.

9

SALES STRATEGIES AND CHALLENGES

You might have noticed by now that I use the word "connect" a lot. Let me explain what I mean by that. When you connect with someone, your interactions with them go deeper than surface level. You move from talking about mundane things like the weather and onto subjects that make you feel happy, excited or stimulated. When you connect with someone, you accept who they are and they, in turn, accept you. You'll feel mutual admiration for each other and form a relationship that can last long term.

A lot of the advice I share in this book is intended to help you better connect with your buyers and people in general. Even if you are an introvert, you can learn how to deeply connect with people you meet. It begins with you, making the decision that from this point forward, you will open yourself up to forming greater relationships with people by doing things that make people feel good when they are in your presence.

Connecting with someone doesn't mean that you have to exchange phone numbers and hang out every weekend! A good connection can be formed and enjoyed for five minutes or for five decades. Have you ever met a stranger at a random place that made you laugh and brought out your inner beauty for just a few minutes? That's a great example of connecting with someone, though briefly.

People want to feel important, even important people. You connect with people by making the conversation about them. The best way to do this is to ask questions, listen more and talk less. When we listen, we learn.

People are so fascinating when we take the time to get to know them. People are like onions; they are made up of multiple layers. With each layer that you dig through, you learn something new. For example, when I met an artist named Bill Jordan, I just thought he was a regular guy doing regular things. It seemed that we didn't have much in common. But then, during a conversation it was revealed that he had studied sacred geometry decades ago. We weren't so different after all. I felt even more connected to him, though, after he told me about his travels through Bali when he studied under a guru. Now, I had an admiration and connection with him that ran deep, because I, too, have a love for travel and studying the same interests.

Learn to love people and see who they really are behind their public facade. If you can get in the habit of feeling love and acceptance for people, while interacting with them, they will respond back to you with the same.

What does love and acceptance have to do with selling art? A lot. People buy from people they love. For someone to love and accept you, it has to be reciprocal. Love and acceptance is never a one-way street.

What I mean by love is this: have the feeling of love in your body when you are talking with them. That feeling is hard to describe, but you can compare it to how you feel when you are playing with a cute puppy or someone's baby. The feeling is admiration, acceptance and wonder. You can generate this feeling anytime by looking for positive aspects about the person, focusing on those aspects and allowing yourself to feel appreciation for them.

But, you might be thinking, how do you get to a deep connection when you are just meeting someone for the first time, especially when they are possible buyers of your art?

Ask WHO, WHAT WHERE, WHEN, HOW questions that will get your buyers talking about themselves. Don't ask "yes or no" questions, as they can be conversation stoppers. For example, ask:

"Where are you from?"
"What about this piece appeals to you?"
"Why did you decide to come here on vacation?"
"How many other pieces of original art have you collected?"

Find a hook, something that you can relate to with the person. Even if the person is very different from you, you can always find something in common. Love for a particular sport or team, or vacation spot or even a TV show.

For me, if the buyer is a woman with children, I'll ask questions that will connect me with her better, such as:

"How many children do you have?"
"How old are they?"

Since I'm a mother, I can find things to relate with other mothers. Any mother of a teenage girl can laugh and talk about how difficult teenage girls are!

For those of you who love sports, like football or baseball or basketball, if the buyer is also a sports fan, talk about that. If you can get to know your buyer on a deeper level, you can earn their trust and form a long term relationship.

REJECTION DOESN'T EXIST

Never allow yourself to feel rejected. It's not a rejection when people don't buy. It doesn't mean that your art isn't good enough. It means that the person isn't ready for you yet, or they don't get what you're doing, or they don't need it right now.

Sometimes people won't understand what it is that you do. Be kind and gentle about this; most people are not visionaries. You can't blame them if they don't recognize your ideas or your art as the next earth-shattering thing.

The Beatles were turned down by nearly every record label in Europe before landing a record contract with EMI in 1962. Everyone said they wouldn't make it.

J.K. Rowlings, author of the wildly popular *Harry Potter* series, was turned down by dozens of publishers before she got her first book published.

It's painful to be told that your art isn't wanted. The word "no" cuts like a knife right into your healthy psyche. Chews you up and spits you out. Makes you feel less worthy and bitter, if you let it. *Don't let it.*

View each "no" as a temporary thing. A NO will turn into a YES when the timing is right, if you are there when it happens.

LOOK FOR YOUR PEOPLE

My wise husband Drew always says "Some people are going to love your art, and some people are going to hate it. Your job is to find the people who love it."

It's hurtful not being accepted into certain groups or turned away from something that you felt in your heart was so perfect for you.

Drew and I spent years trying to bang down doors in the surf industry of people who didn't quite understand his art. We finally have come to accept that we needed to skip the closed doors and go through the doors that were wide open to us. There are many people who are a match with our work and our life mission. And we now put our efforts into getting to know those people instead.

We learned this lesson a few years ago when a charity partner broke our hearts. We had helped them raise hundreds of thousands of dollars over the course of a few years. We had worked very closely with them, donating our time and art to their cause. Then one year they held an art exhibit of "the top artists in surf." We were shocked to find that Drew was excluded from the event. We thought it was a mistake, since Drew was one of the most influential artists in surf. When we asked why, we were told that the committee felt that Drew didn't fit into a show that had a lot of "hip" artists. We didn't know what they meant by that. Drew is just a regular guy that surfs big waves and paints for a living. He doesn't dress fashionably or try to make a statement. And that was where he didn't fit in. We felt used and let down.

That experience helped me learn to accept the hard truth that our brand and style is not going to be a match for everyone. We have our people, and they love us. And the other people, well, they have their own thing going on and we just don't fit in. And that's okay.

Remember that you and your creations are worthy and that there are many opportunities lining up to accept you and your art right now. You just have to look in the right places to find them. Don't give up when you're pushed away. Keep looking for the perfect match. Be patient.

DON'T SELL ICE TO AN ESKIMO

There's an old saying that says that if you're good at sales, you could sell ice to an Eskimo. But that's not fair, why would you waste an Eskimo's money on something they don't need!

Keep your integrity. Never sell something to someone that isn't right for them. It will harm your reputation and that's not worth the money you'll make from the sale.

Turn away projects that are not for you. When someone wants to commission Drew to paint a portrait, we tell them no, Drew is not a portrait painter. Sure, he could paint a portrait, but it won't be the best one. Instead, we refer them to a friend who does a great job of painting portraits.

Take the time to find out what your customer needs, ask questions, listen intently, care about what they have to say. And then sell them what they need or refer them out to someone who can give it to them.

IF YOU'RE DESPERATE TO MAKE A SALE TODAY

Art sales ebb and flow. Some months art sales will be prosperous and other months will be so lean you'll ask yourself why you decided to do this for a living! Money fluctuations are especially hard on those of us who formerly worked a real job and got used to a steady pay check.

For Drew and I, art sales are slowest in the months of January and September. Sometimes we find ourselves in serious need of a CASH INFUSION. This "desperation" to sell art actually works in our favor, because it forces us to take deliberate action, which leads to growth.

My quickest remedy for slow sales is to get on the phone and start calling people. I begin with calling collectors who have bought from us in the past. I'll ask how they are doing. I'll listen and converse and then ask if there is anything they need from us right now.

Next I'll call on people who have shown interest in the past but never bought. I'll say "Hey, I was wondering if you ever got the artwork you needed. How did it go?" This helps me understand why they decided not to buy from us, and it opens the door to possible work with them in the future. I always ask "Is there anything we can do for you right now?"

Sometimes they will say *no, but thanks for calling.* I'll remind them to keep us in mind for the future. Other times they will say "well, while you're on the phone, yes. I'm working on a new project and need an illustration." Either way, it's great that I called, because it keeps the lines of communication open. People forget about you if you don't keep in touch. Out of sight, out of mind.

Let's take a moment to write out who you will call to get a cash infusion. Right now, grab your notebook and write the following lists:

1. Five people who have bought from me in the past
2. Five people I would like to do business with
3. Five local people I can go visit in person

Make a commitment to give this method a try. For the next 30 days, every morning, begin your day by writing a list of five people you will contact by phone or in person. Check it off as you go.

Call and visit a minimum of five potential buyers every day. After a month of this consistent action, you will be shocked at how many wonderful opportunities and commissions come from it.

KEEP LEARNING AND PRACTICING SELLING

Set the intention to learn more techniques to connect with people and sell your work. Read books and blogs on selling and take online courses. Continue learning and practicing until it comes naturally to you.

FOLLOWING UP WITH YOUR BUYERS

Don't wait more than a day to follow up with someone who showed interest in your work. When someone shows interest, by email, in person or any other way, follow up with them within 24 hours. Make sure you've answered their questions and given them the opportunity to say yes.

If you wait longer than 24 hours, you might miss the sale. Art purchases are impulsive and there are many other artists out there that will want the work. If you wait too long, the buyer will lose interest and move on to something else. If you wait even a few days, you'll probably have lost the sale.

Set up a system that helps you remember to call or email someone if they didn't buy after your last interaction with them.

Never assume they don't want to buy if you don't hear back from them. Instead, assume they got busy and need to be reminded. Make it easy for them to buy from you; you should be doing all the work, including making the effort to close the sale. Sometimes when a client doesn't respond right away, there's a good reason, and usually it has nothing at all to do with you.

One of the abstract artists I work with had a situation where her buyer was very interested, and just before the sale was about to happen, the buyer disappeared. The artist was upset and didn't understand. I suggested she continue following up and calling the buyer every few weeks. For months, the buyer didn't even respond. I told the artist to just keep trying. Finally, months later, the buyer resurfaced. He apologized and said that his mother had died and life was upside down for awhile. He was still interested in the painting and thanked the artist for following up with him.

It's your responsibility to follow up with your clients. It is not your client's responsibility to follow up with you. Most people will buy after they have been contacted by you at least seven times. If you give up on a potential client after the first or second follow up, you are losing money.

If, after sending a price quote, you don't hear back within 48 hours, send an email asking "Did you receive my email from two days ago? Please email me back and confirm that you got it." That will prompt a response from them and will reopen the dialog.

If they don't respond to your follow up email, then call them. Don't give up on your clients! Create a reminder system for yourself to follow up with every client, and don't stop trying to reach them until you get a "yes" or a definitive "no" from them. A "maybe" doesn't count. If you get a "maybe" then you aren't finished following up.

I don't ever give up on a sale until the client gives me a definite no. For the last eight months, I've been trying to sell a painting to a Brophy collector. He had bought a painting earlier and when we installed it in his home, I noticed a large, bare wall in his living room. I can't stand a bare wall! We had the perfect piece for this space, a beautiful six foot by eight foot abstract painting in our studio. I took a photo of his wall and later Photoshopped the painting on it and texted him the photo, showing him how perfect the art would look on his wall. He was mildly interested and I invited him to come to the studio to see the painting in person, and he did. He didn't say no to the painting, but he didn't say yes. Every month since then, I sent him a reminder that the painting is waiting for him.

Last month, I got an idea; I offered to install it and give him thirty days to make up his mind. I said "I guarantee that you will love this painting. I'm so sure of it, that if you don't love it in thirty days, I'll come take it back and you will owe me nothing." He still wasn't sure but again, didn't say no. Just last week, I called him again and asked "What is it going to take to get this painting on your wall?" I was so happy to hear his answer. He said "I'm getting some extra money next month, so I'll take it."

I didn't give up on this collector. I was actually having fun seeing what it would take to get him to commit to the artwork. I wasn't attached to any outcome, but I knew in my heart that it was perfect for his space. My job was to get him to see that.

Don't give up on your buyers. Let them decide when they want to say no. If they tell you anything other than a no, that means there is still an opportunity for a sale. And if they *do* tell you no, that's probably temporary. "No" doesn't usually mean no forever, it just means no for now.

Setting up a reminder system will help you stay on track with your follow ups. An easy system is to set reminders on your online or phone calendar. After responding to an inquiry or sending a price quote, add a reminder to your calendar to follow up in two days if you don't hear from them.

In two days, send a follow up email. Then add another reminder to follow up in five days. In five days, if you haven't heard back, call them on the phone. Then add another reminder to follow up again in a week.

If you don't get the sale after these follow ups, then add a reminder to follow up in a month, and start sending them once a month reminders. Sometimes people eventually come around.

Following up until you get a definite answer is not bugging people, it's actually helping them. Many of your clients will appreciate the follow up, as they get busy or distracted by the other things happening in their lives. Since you are the one selling something, it's up to you to make it easy for them.

DO NOT FEEL ATTACHED TO THE OUTCOME OF SELLING

Yes, you want to sell your art, but don't allow yourself to feel attached to having to sell it. I realize this sounds a little counter-intuitive. But, when you feel desperate to sell something, your buyer will sense that. And that's when they won't buy, because something feels strange to them.

Get your mindset into a place so you are okay with any outcome. This way you will relax and be very pleasant to talk with.

BUILD RELATIONSHIPS

All selling is about relationships. Every relationship must be tended to regularly for it to grow. Keep in touch with your past buyers and interested buyers. Implement the following habits for keeping in touch with your buyers:

- Collect email addresses and send out a bi-weekly email with photos of new art that's available. Tell a story for each one.
- Call at least five people a day; call past buyers to ask how they are, and interested buyers to see if there's anything you can do for them.
- Send a thank you and/or holiday card to every buyer of your work.
- Go to events (networking, trade shows, etc.) to meet new people to add to your relationship list.

COLLECT CONTACT INFORMATION

Keep a list of past buyers, fans and potential buyers. You can keep this list in the form of a spreadsheet or on a newsletter list. This will come in handy when you have something new to announce, like a new series or an upcoming event. Build your list by asking people for their emails. Be diligent about recording the contact information as soon as you get it.

Every time a person shows interest in your art, no matter where you are, ask for their name, email address and phone number. Then ask permission to add them to your list of people you send emails to when you have new artworks to show or an upcoming event.

When you do a live event, have a clipboard with a sheet of paper with lines on it and columns for NAME, CITY, STATE, EMAIL. Ask people to add their information to the paper.

We have a lot of random people come into Drew's studio from the busy street we are located on. I keep a clipboard on my desk and I ask every single person to put their information on it. Their names are promptly added to our Mailchimp newsletter account, and they start receiving Drew's newsletter right away.

Be sure to get their permission to add their email to your newsletter list. Without permission, it is considered spamming. You never want to add a name to your email list without permission.

A great suggestion from my friend Owen Garratt is to have what he calls a "drop box." A drop box is a box that you have at a live event. People can put their business card or name and email address in to enter a drawing to win something, like an art print or a coupon for a discount off of your art. This is an effective way to get a lot of names added to your list at once.

I've been collecting emails from Drew's fans and buyers for over ten years. We send out regular newsletters through

Mailchimp and a majority of our sales come from people on that list.

SALES LOVES SPEED

If you want to sell more art, you have to move your sales FAST. The longer a prospective buyer waits on making a purchase, the less likely they will buy. It's your job to move them from "interested" to "sold" quickly.

One way to move the process along is to respond to a buyer quickly, within 24 hours, of them showing interest.

Then, if they don't buy right away because they are waiting to make a decision, ask "Can I call you back tomorrow, and you can let me know what you decided?" Then call them at the scheduled time the next day. Don't let too much time go by, because when you do, the sale usually dies.

STUCK SALE

A stuck sale is when a buyer shows interest, but doesn't make a decision either way. Your goal is to get them to either say yes or no. There shouldn't be a maybe, as a maybe can be forever.

When a sale is stuck, NEVER say to them "I'm just touching base" or "I'm checking in." It's not powerful enough to move the sale. Instead, call and find out where they are stuck. Ask them directly: "Have you made a decision?"

If they say they have not yet made a decision, ask them "Why not? What is concerning you?" Keep asking questions until you have a clear answer as to why they have not decided yes or no.

Once you understand what's stopping them, then you can help move it along. If it's money, give them payment options. If it's another problem, see what you can do to solve it.

One of the artists I coach had a collector interested in one of her large paintings, but dragged it out for months without buying. The artist would call him every few weeks to say "I'm just following up. When can I get this painting to you?" And each time, the buyer would say he still wasn't sure, and ended the conversation with a "maybe". I suggested that she change the questions she was asking. One day she called and asked him, very directly, "I know you love this painting. So what is it that's keeping you from buying it?" He admitted, "I just don't like the frame." Now that the artist had this information, it was so easy for her to remedy it. She offered to swap out the frame for one that he liked. It worked, he gave her a credit card number and it was sold.

The frame was an easy fix. Sometimes, the problem or concern the buyer has is more complicated. Keep asking until you find out what it is. Once you know, tell them that you will give it some thought and get back to them. Then brainstorm a solution.

If pricing is their concern, take the time to see if you can cut back on materials or offer a less expensive option. Once you have created a solution, contact them and say "I've been thinking about what you said, and I have an idea of how to solve that. Let's get back on the phone and I'll share it with you."

The trick is to get to the bottom of the issue quickly. Don't let it simmer for weeks or months, as that's how you lose the sale.

UNQUALIFIED BUYERS AND TIRE KICKERS

There are three types of buyers that we encounter in the art business.

1. Your right buyer, who is a viable client and will respond to your quote with a yes or a no.
2. The unqualified buyer, who cannot afford your prices or isn't ready to commit to the project.
3. The tire kicker, who is just curious about your pricing. They never intended to buy anything. No matter what price you give them, they won't buy.

Once we understand which buyer we are dealing with, we can better handle the challenges of selling to them. Below are some of the challenges we encounter with buyer type #2 and #3.

Challenge #1 - Emailed the client a quote and they disappeared:

Don't you hate it when you email a price quote to someone and then they never respond? There are ways to remedy this. But first, it helps to know that out of all the people asking for price quotes through email, about 50% of them are tire kickers, 25% are unqualified buyers and only 25% are our right buyers.

Often we assume that price was the reason they didn't respond. But that's not always the case. There are other reasons someone didn't respond to your email. Some are:

1. They never received your email (it went into a spam folder or got lost).
2. They got busy and forgot about it.
3. They didn't have all their questions answered, and then got busy and forgot about it.
4. They were an unqualified buyer.
5. They were a tire kicker and had no intention at all of buying.
6. They had some other reason, and it's your job to find out what that reason is.

There are few ways to remedy these deal killers. The easiest is by talking with them. You can significantly cut down on the number of people who don't respond to your email price quotes by vetting them through live conversation.

When you receive an email from someone who is asking for a price quote, ask to set up a phone call first. Tell them that you want to get a clear understanding of what they need so that you can give a proper price quote.

This will make the tire-kickers go away because tire kickers do not want to talk to you. They only want your pricing. They most likely will disappear as soon as you email them a question or ask to talk to them. Good riddance! They are time wasters.

Most serious buyers will happily set up a time for a phone call. At worst, they will email you back and ask that you interact digitally. (If you can get them on the phone, that is best. But, if they insist on email or texting, then give them what they want.)

When you get them on the phone, ask questions and get clarity on what they want. Form a friendly bond through conversation, and then send a price quote based on your new understanding.

When you send a price quote, even if it is an informal email quote, make sure it includes the answers to any questions the client might ask. Size, medium, how many, timing, etc.

Follow up within 48 hours. Your follow up should be short and sweet. Say "I'm following up on my price quote from two days ago. Did you receive it?" Just asking one simple question will encourage them to hit reply and answer.

Follow up is where most artists blow it. They send a price quote and a month goes by before they decide to find out why the client hasn't bought yet. By then, it's too late.

If you don't hear back from the client with a yes or a no in one week, follow up again with a call. Ask them if they accept your offer. If they say yes, tell them what the next step is (i.e. send an installment payment). If they say no to your offer, this is your opportunity to find out why and see what you can do to push it along.

Sometimes people will just disappear. You can't get them to answer an email and you can't get them on the phone. They were either glorified tire kickers, or things changed for them.

Life got in their way, something bad happened, or their business changed gears. Whatever it is, it's certainly not personal and most likely has nothing to do with you. Let it go.

Challenge #2 - They ask for an unreasonable discount:

An artist told me she had a client demand that she give a 50% discount and make it a rush job, please! Yes, there are people in the world who are unreasonable and downright insulting. You don't have to pander to them.

When you encounter a client like this, handle it with grace while staying firm on your price. Let them know that your pricing is based on a *business model* that you have carefully crafted and you are unable to stray from that. Offer them other options, smaller pieces, less scope of work, or existing art at lower prices that they can purchase. Then, thank them for their time and let it go.

If they never come back to you, consider yourself fortunate. The clients who demand the biggest discounts are always those who are the most difficult to deal with.

Challenge #3 - You blurt out prices that are too low and do work for less than you're worth:

An artist wrote "I just painted two ukuleles for $100. The client told me that's all he could afford. Sometimes I blurt out prices that are too low and get stuck doing a lot of work for little pay. It sucks."

There are two fixes to this very common problem. The first is to have set pricing for what you do. The second is to stand firm on your price, but offer a lower priced alternative to match a lower budget.

When you have established pricing, and a client says "I only have $100 but I want you to paint both of these ukuleles for me," you can say, "For $100, I can paint a beautiful little flower on one of them. If you want both of them painted, it will cost you $_____."

If you give a client a price and they ask if you can do it for less, then offer an alternative that will match the price they are willing to pay. For example, if they want you to create fifty illustrations but can only afford 50% of the amount you would charge, offer to create twenty five illustrations (half) to fit their budget. Or find another way to save you in time and materials so you can lower the price.

Challenge #4 - The client continuously asks for a lower price, even after you agreed to a price:

When someone continuously asks for more and more, at a lower price, don't give in. It's not your responsibility to subsidize their business and their mistakes.

A South American reggae band emailed asking Drew to design their new album cover. We gave a price quote, and the band replied "Oh, we can only pay half of that price."

I came up with a lower priced option to meet their budget, one that would take Drew half the time to create. I emailed the band and told them that we could meet their budget with a more simple design.

They disappeared for three months. I continued to follow up, and finally one day they emailed and said "We hired another artist to do the work. We paid him money and then he disappeared!" I told them that Drew is still available, and are they ready to get started? They responded back that now that they spent money on that other artist, they wanted an even cheaper deal! Of course, by this time, I was not happy. We had already wasted several hours on them.

Some people just aren't viable clients. Don't waste too much time on them. Let them go.

10

MULTIPLE STREAMS OF INCOME

An effective way to make a good living with your art is to implement multiple streams of income through different sales channels.

What I mean by income streams is that you set up many different places and ways to sell your art, rather than relying on just one sales channel.

For example, artists that were selling solely through galleries ten years ago suffered a massive income loss when huge numbers of galleries went out of business after the economic crash of 2008. But the artist who sold through galleries as well as their own online store, art fairs, art lessons and various other sales channels were able to survive the great crash.

I read once that wealthy people have seven different income streams. I always think about that, and I'm constantly looking for new income streams to add to our art business.

Drew and I sell his work through a multitude of channels. This way if one dries up, we have the others to fall back on.

This was helpful for us when the economy crashed in 2008. We watched as many other small businesses closed their doors around us.

Some of our sales channels include online sales on www.drewbrophy.com, newsletter mailings to collectors, galleries, licensing to manufacturers, Amazon.com, open houses in our studio, live painting events and commissioned illustration projects.

Think of different channels where you can sell your art and then begin implementing them one-by-one. Master one area first, and then once you have it automated and running easily, add another and another.

RESTAURANTS AND PUBLIC PLACES

Beware of wasting your time and money trying to sell art where art doesn't sell. Art will not sell in any place where there isn't someone dedicated to sell it. Take, for example, a restaurant. To sell art, someone has to be there, in the flesh, working to sell art. Most restaurants are not interested in selling your art, as they are focused on running their own business. And, most likely, your art will be damaged by food splatters, heat or customers. A restaurant is not a gallery. I would also steer clear of coffee shops, libraries and juice bars.

The exception to this is if you are having an art exhibit at a restaurant or public venue. If you are there at all times to sell the art, then it will sell. But don't leave your art on loan at one of those places for an undefined period of time; you might get your artwork back damaged and unsellable.

Another exception is a restaurant that is known for selling art. A good friend of ours, artist Thomas Davis, owns the fine dining destination called Collector's Cafe in Myrtle Beach, South Carolina. They are one of the few restaurants in the country that specializes in fine food and fine art, and they sell both very well.

Find venues where you can set up your work and where your target market, your buyers, will be. Be there and engage with your buyers. They want to meet the artist.

To effectively sell art you have to get it in front of large numbers of people, analyze what sells and what doesn't, and over time, make adjustments accordingly. You have to experiment with different sales channels. What works for one artist might not work for another.

When you hit on something that is working, pump it up even more. Put more energy and time and money into it. When something isn't working, discontinue it and move onto the next strategy.

11

HOW TO MAKE MONEY WITH LIVE EVENTS

One income stream for artists is through creating at live events. You can get paid to paint at corporate parties, while promoting your work!

Large companies hold annual corporate meetings at luxury hotels all over the country. They pay event planning organizations big bucks to put on an exciting party for them. Often included in the entertainment is an artist, who arrives with their canvas and easel and paints the entire time, as an added entertainment for the guests. There are many different types of artists that are hired for these events. Airbrush, oil painters, glass blowers, sculptors, caricature artists and even sand sculpture artists.

One example of a live painting event we did was when Drew was hired to paint a surfboard during a private party at the St. Regis Hotel in Laguna Beach, California. The event planner had set a tropical theme for the party, and a surfboard artist was a perfect fit.

Drew arrived with his surfboard, paint pens and even his own lights, because he knew that most venues don't provide the lighting he prefers. He brought another, finished painting on a surfboard to display, so the guests could see what a finished piece looked like. It was "eye candy" that drew people in, and made his area look professional.

For three hours he painted while talking to guests at the party. Though he wasn't a football fan, even he was impressed by the attendees—in one room almost every single owner of the various National Football League teams was gathered! Alongside them were some of the most famous football players in the country.

The best part was this: Drew was paid well for doing what he loves to do; paint surfboards. And he gained a few new fans that night, too.

The benefits of creating at these events are plentiful:

- You tighten up your skills and get better, faster and more precise as time goes on.
- You gain practice talking to people as you work. This is an important skill to hone, because the more comfortable you become at interacting with others, the better your sales are overall in everything that you do.
- You may meet future collectors of your work.
- It can be a lot of fun.
- You get paid well!

HOW MUCH MONEY CAN YOU MAKE?

You can charge anywhere from $600 to $5,000 and in some cases more, for a 3-4 hour event. Now we have standard pricing that we charge for events where Drew paints a surfboard; prices start at $4,500 for up to three hours, plus set up and tear down time. A three hour event can take a total of five hours. The $4,500 that we charge includes the surfboard and surfboard stand, which the client gets to keep. If the client wants more items such as art prints or giveaways, we charge extra for that as well.

For full day events we charge Drew's day rate plus expenses. Last year we were hired for a 4-day event and were paid $12,000 plus travel fees. The company that hired us for that event was a luxury car company and they wanted Drew to provide the highest quality surfboards, which required longer hours. Each event and company has different requirements and we take those details into account when pricing it out.

The range of what you can charge may seem vast, but there are a few factors that determine the amount:

- Geographic Location – some areas are more expensive than others (in big cities such as NY, CA, Miami, you can charge on the high end).
- Famous/well-known artists – can charge more than those who are not well-known.
- The event planning company that hires you – the General Contractors and Destination Management companies – are often able to pay you more than a small company

that specializes in sending out talent to parties. This is because the smaller companies tend to work directly with the event planning companies, and so there's a middleman that cuts into the profits.

In the beginning, you may need to charge on the lower end, but once you have two to three references and have shown yourself to be reliable, you can command payment on the higher end. When we started doing this we charged $1,500 plus expenses per event. But, now that we are pros at it, we charge much more.

WHO KEEPS THE ARTWORK CREATED AT THE EVENT?

You get to keep your painting after the event, and sell later, enabling you to make money off of that piece again. Or, you may offer it for an additional fee to your event client, or include it in your overall fee, which is what we do.

You always retain the copyrights to your work, regardless of who buys the original, unless you sign your rights away in a separate agreement.

Typically you will be hired by the company planning the event. They are either a General Contractor of events or a Destination Management Company, hired by the company who is hosting the event.

For example, a Fortune 500 company will hold various events throughout the year, in different locations, for their top salespeople or customers.

Rather than handle the event planning themselves, they would hire a General Contractor who specializes in event management. That General Contractor would then hire the caterer, the bartenders, and you.

You will directly charge the event planner and then they will bump your price up by about 15-20% when they "sell" you to their client; this is where event planners make their money. Once their client commits, they will let you know and ask for a confirmation of the date. Be sure to respond immediately.

Then, send them a written agreement. Ours is titled "Live Artist Demonstration–Confirmation Agreement." Ask them to send your 50% installment payment to hold the date, and put it on your calendar.

The remaining balance is due to all of the vendors (and you) the evening of the event. They should have a check waiting for you in a nice little envelope. A few days before the event, send an email reminder to have your check waiting for you.

HOW TO GET HIRED FOR LIVE EVENTS

Contact event planners in your area, or the nearest big city, to show them what you offer. An emailable brochure in a pdf is the best way, or, a link to a website that describes what you offer.

Your PDF or web page should contain the following:

- A description of what you're offering: to do live paintings (or creating, or sculpting, etc.) at events.
- A short description of your method of painting or your niche, and your medium.

Drew's niche is surf art, so we offer to send him to paint a surfboard at beach-themed events. If you have a niche, that's your selling proposition.

If you don't have a specific niche, that's okay. Most of the artists that paint at these corporate events are painting landscapes or other local scenes on canvas.

- Describe what makes you unique and why it will be interesting to their guests.
- Include photos of you painting, your art and if you have them, of you painting at events.
- For an added bonus: Include optional ancillary items that the client can purchase for the guests attending. Pricing should be between $5 - $50 per item. (i.e. glass-blown starfish, 5" x 5" matted prints, hand-made rose sculptures, stickers, etc.)
- Include your name, phone number and other contact information on every page of the brochure – make it easy for them to reach you.
- Your pricing should be on a page that can be emailed separately from the photos so that the event planner can email your photos/brochure to their client.

HOW TO FIND EVENT PLANNERS

The best way to reach event planners is through direct solicitation via e-mail and phone calls. Send your information to the Account Managers, as they are the people who pull together all the details for the party host.

You can find event planners by doing an online search of the following key words:

1. DESTINATION MANAGEMENT COMPANY
2. GENERAL CONTRACTORS FOR EVENTS
3. EVENTS PRODUCTION

Then send an introduction e-mail that is short and to the point. It should mention that you are available for events and that you would like them to consider you for future clients. Include your PDF brochure and ask them to call should they have any questions.

When you get an Account Manager on the phone from an event company, ask them questions to help you understand what their needs are. Here are a few:

What do you look for when contracting with an artist?

Who are your main clients? What type of companies?

What seems to be the most popular theme of the events you do?

Who are some of your best artists that you've hired, and what made them the best?

What can I do to make your job easier?

HOW TO GET HIRED OVER SOMEONE ELSE

According to one event planner that I have done a lot of work with, event planners are looking for the following items when hiring an artist for an event:

1. Reliability is number one. The event planners have a tough job pulling together everything for a big night. They re-hire the artists that they can count on to be on time and do a great job.

2. A clearly understood brochure, pamphlet or email describing what the artist does. There should be prices and photos of the art, the artist making the art, and if possible, of the artist at events.

3. Ancillary Items that the artist offers for purchase that can be given to guests at the event.

4. A people-person; someone who can talk to the guests.

5. A self-starter: someone who can show up, set up, get it done, tear it down and ask for very little help from the planners.

Affordable Price: Never made it on this list. It's apparently not the most important thing.

Always use a written agreement to ensure that your client/event coordinator is agreeable to your payment terms. It can be a simple, one-page form that outlines the details.

Event Details listed on the agreement should include:

Where and when the event will take place, phone number of the contact person you will meet at the event, what time the artist should arrive.

Pricing: The Agreement should include your price, how many hours you will create at that price, an additional fee for travel, and any optional items that you offer. (Be sure to add travel expenses for events outside of your area.)

Payment Guidelines: Your payment guidelines should be made clear. Indicate that you require a non-refundable installment payment up front to hold the date and when final payment is payable (the day of the event).

(Visit www.mariabrophy.com for a proposal template in my How to Make Money Painting at Live Events package.)

WHILE AT THE EVENT

Arrive early and set up your area with little disruption to the event planners. At this point, they will be running around like chickens with their heads cut off, stressed and wildly getting things ready before the guests arrive. Be as helpful as possible.

Generate excitement in the physical area in which you are placed during the event. Create a vibe around you that says "welcome, come see what I'm painting." Make people feel compelled to watch you paint.

Be open, happy and friendly. Appear genuinely interested in the people who come up and talk with you. Bring an extra painting, finished and framed and placed on an easel. (Get permission from the host first and make sure there's room for what you're bringing.) We usually bring a painted surfboard in a stand, which creates a terrific atmosphere. Also bring a small, framed biography about yourself that can be placed on a table.

If you are planning to paint something just for this event, paint it in the theme of the party and if you can, incorporate something subtle about the company in the painting. We often do this, and when we do, it entices the company to want to buy the painting.

If it's a "shy" crowd, get them interested. Some crowds are fun and lively, but others can be tough. If you find yourself in a group where you're feeling invisible and no-one's coming to see your work, then put yourself out there and draw them in. After all, that's what you were hired to do—to entertain and be an addition to the event.

To engage the guests at an event, be very friendly and smile and ask:

"What do you think of the painting?"
"Are you enjoying the party?"
"Where are you from?"

Or Drew's personal favorite, "Hey, you want to finish this painting for me?"

A little humor helps in every situation!

OTHER MONEY MAKING OPPORTUNITIES WITH LIVE EVENTS

You can use these guidelines for other types of events, too, such as:

RETAILER EVENTS: Align yourself with a manufacturer that makes a product that can be customized during an in-store event.

An example is when Drew teamed up with Converse to paint Chuck Taylors at several Nordstrom locations.

The service you provide is making the retailers' customers happy and it's an event that creates press and energy for the manufacturer as well.

TRADE SHOW BOOTHS: If you are aligned in a specific industry (example: equestrian, snowboarding, scuba-diving, motor cross, agriculture, medical, etc.), seek to get paid to paint live in the tradeshow booth of a manufacturer.

Your live painting will create energy and excitement in the booth of your client, and that will bring them more business. It's a win-win for all!

CHARITIES: Some charities will pay for your live painting at their gala events. Find charities that do black-tie events in your area and see if they have the funds to pay for your presence.

12

PRESENTING YOUR WORK

*"Most of the fine art industry is
ignoring independent artists."*

—Cory Huff,
author of *How to Sell Your Art Online*.

Before you present your work to the world, it's best to have a
series of works to display. A series would be a unified, cohesive
body of work in one theme that is a representation of an idea,
concept or experience.

Examples of a series of work:

- Visionary artist Alex Grey did a series of twenty one
  paintings called the Sacred Mirrors Series. The series
  visually describes a process of transformation from body
  awareness through sociopolitical awareness to spiritual
  awareness.
- Photographer Larry Beard shot a beautiful series of San
  Clemente sunsets each day for 365 days in a row.

- Drew Brophy painted a series of twelve paintings titled Exploring Sacred Geometry.

Having a cohesive series prepares you to exhibit your work in a gallery, show or event. It also helps the viewer to understand a concept, idea or thought that inspired the series.

If you don't have a unified series of work to show, then you need to go back to the studio and get it done. It doesn't have to be complicated like Alex Grey's. It could be as simple as "Life in Cape Cod" or "Elephants on Parade" or "Red and Blue Abstracts."

You never want to exhibit a hodge-podge of artworks that have no synergy. If you have been dabbling in landscapes, dog portraits and punk rock art, you don't want to show all of those mixed together. It will confuse the viewer and give mixed messages that will not result in sales.

Instead, display a consistent theme or medium, something that ties all of your works together as a whole. This will make a clean presentation and attract buyers.

13

LIVE SELLING

When I was in the insurance industry, we used the phrase "get out and press the flesh" often. We knew that no matter how many flyers we mailed or advertisements we placed, the best way to sell was to get out and meet people in person.

To sell your work, you have to get it out in front of people, go outside of your comfort zone and meet people.

Maybe you're thinking that you want to only sell your work online. Selling online is good, but it's just one piece of the puzzle. It will only get you so far. **If you want to see your career take a quantum leap, you need to get out of your workspace and show your work, live.**

Live selling is crucial to your growth as an artist. You can develop life-long relationships with buyers when you meet them in person. This is key for long term income growth. You also get instant feedback on what is going to sell and what isn't, and you ask people their opinion on the spot. With that feedback, you can quickly make corrections and adjust your offering.

LIVE SALES CHANNELS

Art fairs and festivals: Two friends of mine, Hannah and Nemo (artbynemo.com), left their professional jobs years ago to focus on creating and selling art. They sell their work exclusively through festivals throughout the U.S., traveling in their RV and living an adventurous lifestyle.

You can earn a great living exhibiting at the better festivals. Some festivals focus only on fine art, some on arts and crafts. Choose the ones that fit with your long term goals. Do an online search for fairs and festivals across the country. Some are good for sales, some are not. Figure out which ones are good by researching, asking other artists, and by trial and error.

Trade Shows: Sell your work at one of the thousands of trade shows happening all over the country.

For example, Owen Garratt, an artist from Canada, has had great success selling his oil rig drawings to the executives at oil industry trade shows. If your work would appeal to interior designers and architecture firms, you might exhibit at a design show such as West Edge Design Fair in California. If your work would appeal to the Cannabis industry, exhibiting at the Champs trade show might be good for you.

Think of what market your work would fit in, and find a trade show in that industry. There are many art industry trade shows to consider, such as the Art and Frame Expo and the Art Expo New York.

The downside to having your own booth at a trade show is the high expense. You can spend anywhere from $5,000 to $20,000 to cover your booth costs and travel expenses.

But, there are ways around that. The way I like to do trade shows is by getting someone else to pay for us to be there. Find an exhibitor that has a mission and products that align with your work, then offer them value to have you in their booth doing a live painting or decorating their space, and in return, you get paid and/or get to show and sell your work.

Private Home Shows: In my small town of San Clemente, California, there is a very talented and well loved oil painter named Rick Delanty. He's also a dear friend and mentor of mine and Drew's. Rick has been holding shows for twenty years in his own home. Every year, he and his wife transform their home into a gallery and hold a weekend art exhibit. He sells many of his beautiful oil paintings at the show each year. One of the contributing factors to their success is being consistent and holding their show every year at the same time. He's built up a strong collector base and his fans and collectors look forward to it.

If you don't have a home that is big enough to transform into a beautiful gallery space, then ask someone else to host your show in their home. You could gift them with a beautiful art print reproduction or a painting as a thank you.

Live painting at tourist locations: One of the best art books on selling that I ever read is called *Breaking into the Art World* by Brian Marshall White. It's a self-published book and written from the artist's heart, sharing his tried and true method of earning a living with his art. The book is a bit outdated now, but worth a read if you live in a tourist location.

White has earned a living selling paintings and reproductions through the Hawaii tourist market by setting up his work outside of busy restaurants and stores. He would strike a deal with the owner of the business to be able to set up his easel and paint outside their entrance. His live painting would bring more people to the business, which was of great value to them. And, the tourists would marvel at watching him paint and want to buy his originals and matted art prints. This method works great in high traffic tourist areas.

Cooperative Galleries: A cooperative gallery is one that is owned and operated by artists. Every member artist contributes time and money to keep the gallery running. As part "owner" of the gallery, each member artist has a democratic say in how it runs. If you don't have a cooperative gallery in your town, consider starting one.

Group Art Exhibit: Exhibiting your artwork along with other artists at a group exhibit will expose you to many new collectors, as all of the artists together will draw a larger crowd. A group art exhibit can be held anywhere, it doesn't have to be a gallery. You can rent a space for a month or strike a deal with a local business owner that has plenty of space to host a group exhibit. Real estate offices and banks make great hosts as they tend to have beautiful, large spaces and their clientele have money, and, they often are looking for something to make their space the place to be.

Unconventional Places: Be open to the possibility that there are many unconventional ways to sell your work. You will come up with ideas as you brainstorm them. Sometimes the best place to sell your work is right under your nose!

One artist that I work with is a bartender, and her goal is to transition to a full time artist. She sells one or two original paintings every week. Not bad for a part-time artist! I asked "where are you selling it, how are you reaching your buyers, and who are they?" What she told me next just blew me away.

She sells art to the sport fishermen that come into her bar. When she mentions that she's an artist, many will ask "What do you paint?" That's her cue to bring up images on her phone and show them. At that point, someone will ask "how much would that piece cost?" She answers, they arrange for delivery the next day, and boom—sold!

This artist hit on a winning formula. She is in a location that attracts her buyers (sport fishermen), she has their undivided attention (they are relaxing at the bar, having a beer), and she sells art that is perfect for them (fishermen love fish).

You could say this artist is lucky. I say she's brilliant. Many artists wouldn't try to sell art in this way; they would be too shy to show photos or even mention that they are an artist. And if they did, many wouldn't follow up the next day with the potential buyer, thus losing the sale.

This artist's success comes from the following:

- MARKET: Knowing who her Right Buyer is (fishermen with money to buy art)

- LOCATION: Being in a place where her target market gathers (a bar that caters to sport fishermen)
- PREPARATION: Knowing her prices in advance and being prepared to show photos
- SELLING: Presenting her art to them in a friendly, non-pushy way
- FOLLOW UP: Quickly following up and delivering the art the next day

What impressed me the most was that this artist wasn't afraid to take the opportunity to sell her art in the most unconventional of ways.

This method of selling her work gave her immediate feedback as to which images and sizes sell the best. Now she can take this success and grow it exponentially by exhibiting at boat or fishing events, where she will reach larger numbers of her right buyers. She can start collecting emails from her fans and grow her sales through newsletter mailings and online sales as well.

EXERCISE: Grab your pen and paper and brainstorm three unconventional ways to sell your art, using the above examples as inspiration:

1.
2.
3.

Now, write down one concrete step that you will take towards one of the ideas you wrote above:

Now, write down when you will take that step. Give a specific date and commitment:

SCRIPTS FOR LIVE SALES

There are some very simple things you can do to create a better art-selling atmosphere. Below are prompts and scripts that will help you to interact successfully with buyers at a live venue.

Always greet every single person as they enter. This gives them a warm feeling of belonging.

When they leave, thank them for coming. The idea is to make people feel welcome so that they have fond memories of being there.

Converse by asking open-ended questions to get them talking about themselves. Never assume, based on the way someone looks, how much they can afford to spend on art.

Talk less and listen more. Say things like:

"Welcome, thank you for coming. Where are you folks from? What are your names?"

Reply, "glad to have you here, Renee and Joe." Say their names out loud right away so you connect on a personal level (and to help you remember their names).

Or, if you know the person, say: "Welcome, I'm so glad that you came! Have a look at the art and I'll check on you in a while to answer your questions. Enjoy."

You can also ask, "How did you hear about this event?" This helps you know which of your ads or efforts got people there.

To get them talking about themselves, and also have some insight into what kind of art they like, you can say, "Tell me about some of the art you have collected."

Ask them which of your pieces is their favorite. If the piece is not too large, pick it up and place it into their hands. Point out something they should notice. "Look at the fine detail" or "See how it shimmers in the light" or "Look at how well it is printed." By placing it in their hands, you are helping them to feel ownership of it.

If they show great interest in a piece, don't take them away from that one to show them other options. You will confuse them and lose momentum (and probably the sale). Stay right there with the one they want, and don't move away from it until they either buy it, or decide they want to look at others.

Here are some more questions you can ask:

"Why does this piece appeal to you?"

"Where do you envision it hanging, in your home or work space?"

"Tell me about the wall you will hang it on."

Then ask for the sale. Most art sales are lost because the artist forgot to ask for the sale! Don't let the customer leave without giving you a yes or a no. Don't accept a maybe. When someone shows interest in a piece, assume the sale and ask them:

"Do you want to take this home today?"

"Will you be taking this with you or would you want me to ship it to you?"

"Do you prefer to pay by cash or credit card?"

Part of the work of selling art is handling objections. Don't take the first no for an answer. Find out what is really troubling them. Often, we think it's the price, and many times we are wrong.

If someone is showing interest but won't commit, ask them why. "If you love it so much, why don't you take it home today?" This simple question will help you get to the heart of their hesitation, and once you know what that is, you can find a solution to it.

If they say it's out of their budget, ask "If I make it more affordable, would you buy it?" And then offer monthly payments. Get a 25% down payment and let them make monthly payments to pay off the rest. They can take the art home with them right away, so they are excited about their purchase.

If they say they aren't sure it's the right color or if it will fit the space, offer to take it back in a week if it doesn't work for them. If they say they have to check with their spouse or another person, encourage them to text a photo right away and get an answer.

If they ask for a better deal, and you are tempted to give them one, say "I'll tell you what; I'll cover the sales tax for you. Does that sound good?"

Don't let anyone haggle your prices on the actual artwork, as that lowers the value and it's not fair to your previous collectors.

Some artists offer a special "collector's discount" for existing collectors who already own a piece of your work. If you choose to do this, tell them that after they buy their first piece from you, they are now considered a collector. Collectors get a 10% discount on all pieces they buy after the first one.

If they say, "we need to think it over" ask if you answered all of their questions about the piece. If they say yes, then tell them you'll give them a few minutes to think it over. Leave the room and let them have their privacy for a few minutes before returning. When you come back, ask "what did you decide?"

If they say they'll come back later, say "I can't guarantee it will be available later. Most of my work sells quickly." Then ask for their email and phone number, so you can let them know if someone else shows interest in the piece they like.

After a purchase, follow up a week later with a hand written thank you card. Let them know you appreciate them. Keep in contact with all of your collectors through email blasts, holiday cards or occasional phone calls.

14

SELLING YOUR WORK ONLINE

*"Artists can now do practically everything
online that galleries once had to do for them,
and often in much larger ways."*
—Alan Bamburger, ArtBusiness.com

We can thank the internet for the massive shift that artists have experienced in the last decade. Previously, art galleries had the power to make or break an artist's career. Not anymore. The internet has given complete control back to the artist.

When you tell people you're an artist, one of the first things they will ask is where they can see your work. It's convenient to be able to give them a link to a website. If you don't have your own website yet, don't worry. Eventually, you'll want to get your own, but in the meantime, there are other options to display your work online such as social media sites and third party marketplaces.

There are many details to learn when setting up online platforms. The information I share in this chapter is very general. To cover everything on this topic I would have to write another book, and the answers are constantly changing. Before implementing any of the suggestions in this chapter, please go online and do greater research on the topic for the most up to date information.

WATERMARKS ON IMAGES

I cringe when I see a huge, obnoxious watermark stamped across an art image. It not only takes away from the art, it literally ruins it for me.

But shouldn't you place watermarks on your online images? This is a question many artists agonize over. They worry that their work will be stolen or copied. This is a reasonable concern. I've had to fight a few companies over the years who were trying to sell Drew's artwork on their products without permission. To date, I've fortunately been able to stop every single one of them, and one ended up paying us fees for their infringement. But it's a stressful thing to have to deal with.

If your work is good, people are going to copy it. You have to accept that. This is just one part of business that you have to deal with. You can't let your worries stop you from posting your images online. The art business is a visual one; you have to show the world your work for you to be able to sell it.

There are ways to protect your work from copycats and art thieves. The most important is to file copyrights to your artworks. This will give you legal leverage if your work is stolen and being used commercially. I cover this more in the chapter on copyrights.

I recommend placing a subtle copyright notice or your signature or logo or name somewhere on the image, where it's not obstructing the beauty of the art. A few examples of copyright notices are:

"Artwork (c) 2017 Drew Brophy"
"Artwork (c) Drew Brophy"
"(c) Drew Brophy"
"(c) Drew Brophy, all rights reserved."

We have Drew's signature logo placed small in the lower corner of most of his works before posting online. This watermark claims the art as his, which is useful when someone "grabs" the digital image and shares it without giving the artist credit.

For extra protection, you can include in the description posted with the image a copyright notice such as: "Artwork (c) Drew Brophy."

SOCIAL MEDIA

Social media sites are an easy and free way to display and offer your artwork online.

The disadvantage to depending solely on social media, instead of your own website, is that you can't rely on a third party website to stick around or keep things the same. When a third party site changes their algorithm or rules, it can harm your sales. This happened to a lot of people with Facebook. There was a time that anything you posted on your Facebook page was shown in the live feed of the fans who followed you. Then one day Facebook changed it, and now only a very small percentage of your Facebook page followers will see your posts. For the artists who relied on Facebook for marketing, this change lowered their art sales significantly.

The best long-term plan is to have your own website and your own domain name (i.e. www.sarafranklindesign.com). Social media sites are best used as a supplement to your own website. But if you don't have your own website right now, social media sites are great for the short term.

The huge advantage that social media sites offer is the ability to show the world your work and your personality. **Buyers want to know the artist, and social media is a platform that makes a personal introduction.**

The artists that get the most from social media are those who consistently post photos or videos of them creating, sketching and showing their personality. Getting a glimpse behind the daily life of an artist is of great interest to others.

Artists who want to remain private will hurt their sales in today's world. You can't be anonymous and at the same time catch the attention of collectors, not unless you are Banksy. And being anonymous is Banky's thing, so you can't use that idea because it's already taken!

Buyers want to see who you are, not just your art. They want to know what inspires you. They want to see you in action. They want to feel like they know you personally. Social media makes this possible.

If you are new to any social media site, the best way to learn about it is to use it. Watch what other successful artists in your genre are doing and see how they interact with their followers. The only way to truly get value from social media is to use it daily. Be careful, though, not to get sucked into the time warp of social media. Sometimes I'll go online and plan on only posting for five minutes, and the next thing I know, a half hour has gone by! Allow yourself a little bit of time each day, but don't spend hours on it when you should be creating art instead.

FACEBOOK

If you were going to choose only one social media site to display your work, I would recommend a Facebook business page, especially if your buyers are over the age of thirty. Facebook might be losing favor with those under thirty, but it's still one of the best ways to allow friends, family and new fans to see your art and leave comments, giving instant feedback. You can set up "albums" with photos of your artwork, divided by series or themes so people can easily view your work. For example "Barnyards" and "Farm animals" and "Rivers." The albums are a great tool for showing new prospective buyers what you have done in the past, in an organized fashion.

Set up a public Facebook business page for your art, not a private one, as you want to make sure anyone who is interested in seeing your art can do so just by looking it up and not having to "friend" you. Your Facebook business page would be set up in addition to your private/personal page. With a Facebook page, you'll also have the option to "boost posts" or pay for advertising, to put your art in front of people you choose with specific targeting.

Facebook also has a great live streaming video feature that gets a lot of views. Facebook controls the algorithm that allows your fans to see what you've posted, and for live streaming videos, they have set it so that most every one of your followers will see it in their live feed. We have experimented with live videos of Drew painting and it has gained huge numbers of new followers, when his existing followers share it. At the time of this writing, a live stream video on Facebook gets triple the views of a static post. Of course, Facebook could change that at any minute, so use it while it's hot!

OTHER SOCIAL MEDIA SITES

Instagram and Pinterest are excellent for artists to show their work as well. Some artists are using these platforms as an online portfolio, posting new works daily.

We have had a lot of success with selling art on Instagram. Our formula is to post pictures of Drew working on a painting and telling people to call, text or email if they are interested in buying it. When the painting is finished we post the final image. Often, the paintings sell before they are finished.

Take the time to learn how to use proper hashtags on your posts. A hashtag is a word that people use to find what they are looking for, with the "#" symbol. For example, with Drew's sacred geometry art, I would use hashtags such as #sacredgeometryart, #metatronscube, #ancientwisdom, #modernart. If someone is on Instagram, looking for sacred geometry art using a hashtag, they will find Drew's posts more easily.

There are many other social media sites as well, and by the time this book is on the market, there will be new ones that I have not yet heard of. Try out a few and see what works best for you. Focus only on one or two or three. Don't try to use them all, because it will take you away from the most important work, which is creating art.

ONLINE CAMPAIGN SERIES

One way to generate sales in your work online is by posting the making of a series. There are a million ways to do this, so you have to brainstorm what works best for your style, theme and market.

An online campaign will generate great interest in your work and will attract new and existing buyers. It's a very affordable (free) way to market your artwork and get greater exposure.

Choose a number of days that you will commit to the campaign, and then announce it. Daily post photos of the work with a description. When you do this consistently, you will get great results.

For artists who create works with your hands, you would post works in progress. For a painter, each day you would post a sketch of what you're painting that day or week. You would tell a story about it and then post work-in-progress photos. You would mention that the pieces are for sale and give contact information on how to reach you to purchase it. Include photos of you creating, as well. Enlist a family member to get regular shots while you work.

If you're a landscape painter, you might do a series titled "Twenty bridges in Madison County" or "Thirty Days of Louisiana Sunsets" or "Ten weeks in the life of a Tree Hugger".

If you are a photographer or digital artist, you can do the same but instead of posting progress photos you would simply post one image a day and sell limited edition art prints of each. A photographer might post "Thirty days in the desert" and a digital artist might post "Thirty faces of outrageous super heroes."

Series postings can get slow responses at first, but as each day goes on, you will find that it will gain momentum as you continue to stay consistent. People will start to pay attention and follow your progress. People will become inspired, intrigued and impressed that you are doing such a series. And, best of all, you grow exponentially as an artist when you place demands and deadlines on yourself.

In the fall of 2015 our business was slow and we needed an infusion of cash fast, so we decided to have Drew do fifty paintings in fifty days. Every single day he started and finished a small painting. Every single day we sold the painting. Only one painting didn't sell during the fifty days. Due to the high demand for some of the images, we started offering paper prints of the paintings in a limited edition of 20 each. By the end of the fifty days, we had sold $20,000 in paintings and over $3,000 in art prints which sold for $40 each.

The success of our 50/50 series was due to the following factors:

- Drew committed to starting and finishing a small painting every day for fifty days and never strayed from that commitment.
- We first emailed the work in progress, each morning, to Drew's newsletter list.
- Then we posted the artwork in progress to our followers, which at the time were 12,000 on Instagram and 35,000 on Facebook.
- The paintings were on small canvas board sized 8"x10" or 11"x14" and ranged in price from $250 to $500 each.
- We told a story with every painting. People love stories and over time during the series, got excited to see each day's new post.

The trick to getting sales through social media is to be consistent with your posts, grow your number of followers, post quality pictures, and sell in the price range of your followers.

YOUR OWN WEBSITE

If you have a website with a shopping cart, you need to get high volumes of traffic to that site to sell in high volume. This comes easier to artists who have a large following and a big email list, as you can send out regular emails to drive traffic to your online store. You can also use social media to drive traffic to your store, but with the constantly changing rules on those sites, it's hard to rely on.

If you do not have a large following or email list, hire a Search Engine Optimization (SEO) expert and advertise through Google or Facebook to drive traffic to your site. This is well worth the time and money for artists who have a large body of work to sell. You should also be blogging about topics that your target audience is searching for, so your site shows up in the results.

THIRD PARTY ONLINE GALLERIES

A third party online gallery is a gallery website that sells the art of many artists. The best online galleries do a great job of advertising and sell more art than a brick and mortar gallery would.

Much like in the real gallery world, the best of the online galleries are hard to get into. Many have a jury process and you may or may not be accepted. Some take high commissions, as much as 45%, and it's your responsibility to pack and ship the artwork. Others have monthly fees that you need to pay, regardless of whether or not art has sold.

Paying a commission or monthly fee is entirely worth it, if the online gallery is selling your work. They will do a better job of marketing to a large number of people than many artists could do on their own, as they have the funds and staff to do so.

If you are a creator of fine art and wish to target the higher end market, an online gallery would be worth an experiment. There are many to choose from and new ones popping up every day. Here are just a few that you can look into: paddle8.com, saatchiart.com, moderneden.com, ugallery.com and zatista. com.

THIRD PARTY ONLINE MARKETPLACES

A third party online marketplace is a website where you set up your own "store" using their platform, on their website.

Examples of online marketplaces in operation today are artfire.com, zibbet.com, icraft.com, etsy.com and aftcra.com. There are many, many more.

An online marketplace is different from an online gallery, just as a retail store is different from a brick and mortar gallery. The gallery specializes mostly in hand made fine art, while an online marketplace sells arts, crafts and products.

The advantage to using an online marketplace is that you don't have to pay to set up and run a shopping cart on your own website; they provide the store and an easy set up for you on their site. It's a quick, easy way to get your own store online.

The disadvantage is that you can't predict what the marketplace will do in the future. If you put all of your time and focus on it, and then they shut down, you are back to starting over again. This happened with the briefly popular marketplace, Goodsmiths.com. They launched in 2011. At their peak, they had over 6,000 artist shops on their site. However, due to financial troubles, they shut down in 2014.

An online marketplace tends to be geared towards a mid to lower priced market. You can do high volume sales if you learn how to work it.

One artist I know creates children's digital wall art. He is newly retired from teaching and just started making art a few years ago. In his first year of selling on Etsy.com, he sold about

$25,000 in art prints. By year two he doubled his income and in his third year, he broke $100,000 in sales, selling paper prints!

This particular artist hit on a popular art theme, has his prints priced properly for the market, and learned the ins and outs of getting sales on Etsy. It's the only place he sells his work, and so his entire focus is on growing Etsy sales.

I've experimented with selling Drew's reproductions on Etsy.com and have had some sales, but nothing to brag about. However, we didn't put much time into Etsy, as we are focusing in other areas. Where you place your focus, your sales will grow.

PRINT ON DEMAND

Print on demand websites, also known as POD, enable you to upload your artwork and make it available to be printed on a variety of products. The products include art prints, posters, t-shirts, coffee mugs, stickers and cell phone cases, to name a few.

There are many POD companies to choose from. Three examples are fineartamerica.com, cafepress.com and zazzle.com. Some are producing high quality products, and others are not. You have to test them out to decide for yourself.

The advantage to POD is that you never have to handle the actual printing or shipping of anything. All you have to do is set up your account, upload the art, and generate sales. They do the rest.

The downside is that with some POD websites, you get paid very little, in some cases, only 15% of the sale price of the item. The other disadvantage is that it is hard to control the quality. If you are concerned about the quality of items that your art is printed on, you will need to be careful about which company to do POD with.

There are only a few artists making a good living selling exclusively on POD websites. To do high volume sales, you would use several POD sites, offer a huge library of images and invest a great deal of time driving traffic to your POD store sites.

At the very least, it's fun to see how your art would look on a coffee mug or mouse pad, and these websites make it easy to order items with your art printed on it.

15

WORKING WITH GALLERIES

"The art world is molting - some would say melting.
Galleries are closing; museums are scaling back."
—Jerry Saltz, American art critic

Once upon a time, artists needed galleries to sell their artwork. A select few lucky artists were accepted into the gallery system, and the rest were rejected, left with little to no alternatives to sell their work.

The best galleries would take care of their artists, handling marketing, sales and exhibits. It was a dream relationship for any artist, because as we know, artists want to create art, not sell it.

This system died long before I got into the business of selling art. But it worked for generations of artists before it went down. Maybe that's why this strong need to be taken care of is encoded in most artist's DNA. The desire to have their art discovered by one mythical person or to have their art accepted into a gallery has been passed down through generations.

Today, there is a very small percentage of artists that are making a full time living selling their work through galleries. Most of the artists that exclusively sell their work in galleries are not earning enough to survive.

If you are selling your work exclusively through galleries, and your income goal is $100,000 a year, you would have to sell more than $300,000 in art yearly. Of that, you would pay 50% to the gallery, which is $150,000. Subtract your expenses from your remaining $150,000, which are going to be close to 40% (for permits, framing, art supplies, studio rent, travel, web-designer, computers, software, etc.). After expenses, you're left with about $90,000 before taxes. Yes, there are some artists who sell artwork in the high end market and earn $300,000 in a year. But that's not the norm.

If you plan to sell your work through galleries, be sure to supplement your sales by selling through other channels as well. Let the gallery system be just one of your many streams of income.

There are many benefits to having your work in a gallery. If you get into a good gallery, they will help you to better develop your work. Galleries will host exhibits and expose their large list of collectors to your work. If they are doing their job well, they will sell more of your art than you would on your own.

One thing I like about selling in a gallery is that it provides a physical place to send people. When someone asks "where can I see your work?" you can direct them to the gallery.

The downside is that working with galleries can be costly, particularly if you have big pieces that you have to ship across the country or overseas.

We get many requests from galleries in Hawaii to show Drew's work, however, the cost of shipping art to Hawaii from the mainland is high. Most galleries expect us to cover the cost of creating the art, having it framed, and then shipping it there, and they still keep 50% of the sale price. When we do the math, we find there's little profit in it for us.

We've considered having Drew fly to Hawaii to create an art series, as he likes to paint very large pieces and it would save in shipping. But then there's the expense of hotel, rental car and airfare. Either way you slice it, it's costly.

For every opportunity, we have to look at the expense versus the profit. If the cost of getting art into the gallery is close to the amount we would make when it sells, there is no financial incentive to do it.

In one case, I had a gallery in Hawaii agree to pre-purchase Drew's paintings at wholesale prices. They paid for shipping, too. However, this is rare and most galleries won't buy your work outright. Not unless your work has a long history of sales.

I like showing in galleries that are close to home, as there are no shipping costs and you can control how the art is displayed, as well as keep in constant contact with the owners.

Some artists want to build up their resume by showing they have exhibited their work in many galleries. That's good, but don't go broke doing it. Consider the expenses versus the profit for each opportunity.

You can make a profit selling in galleries, even if they are located far away, if you are selling to a large number of them in one geographical area. I know one California artist who sells his work in over a dozen galleries in Hawaii. He flies there twice a year to create new art and do exhibits. Because he is in many galleries in one area, and his art is selling well, he makes a good profit.

THE LEGAL DEAL WITH A GALLERY

Most galleries will require your work to be provided on a consignment basis. This means that you will not be paid until after the work has been sold. If it doesn't sell after a period of time, then you get the work back.

The typical deal with a gallery is that the artist splits the sales of the work 50/50. You get 50% and the gallery gets 50%. The gallery needs 50% because the cost of having a brick and mortar store is high.

I have worked with galleries who take only 30% or 40%, but they are less common. Some of the galleries in higher rent districts keep 60% of the sale and the artist only gets 40%. I feel that anything over 50% to the gallery is excessive. The only way I would pay over 50% commission to a gallery is if there are guarantees and they are selling in massive volume and we are benefiting as much as they are.

If the artwork you create uses very expensive materials, ask the gallery to agree to a 50/50 split after deducting the cost of the materials. When Drew paints a fine art surfboard, he will pay a surfboard shaper as much as $1,000 for the surfboard before he paints it. If it sells for $5,000, we ask the gallery to pay us 50% of $4,000 and all of the $1,000, which was the cost of having the surfboard made. The split looks like this: Sell price is $5,000. We deduct the $1,000 surfboard cost and add it to our 50% of 4,000 = $3,000 payable to us and $2,000 to the gallery. I have never had a gallery disagree with this.

If your artwork doesn't sell after a period of time, you will be asked to either switch it out for something fresh, or take it back. For a gallery to stay in business, they have to move inventory quickly.

There are good galleries and then not-so-good galleries. The good ones will properly market your work through advertising, newsletters and hosting exhibits. They will advise you on how to improve your work for better sales. They will introduce your work to their large list of collectors. They will have a good consignment agreement that benefits both you and them. They will treat you with respect.

HOW TO GET INTO A GALLERY

If you want to get into a gallery, take the time to research galleries and find those that your work would fit best in. If you are a pop artist, don't attempt to get into a gallery that specializes in impressionistic art. Be sure that your work is congruent with the type of art that the gallery carries.

Before approaching a gallery, be prepared. Read their website thoroughly. Attend their exhibits. Know the names of the people that you need to talk to. Get familiar with the artwork of other artists they represent. Look on their website to see if they have submission guidelines, and if they do, follow their instructions.

Take your time to fully prepare, as it will be appreciated and noticed. If you don't care enough to put in the work, you are wasting both your time and the gallery's time.

Prepare a portfolio of a current series of work in digital format, so that it's easy to show either in person or by email. Don't show art that you did five or ten years ago. They want to see what you are doing now. If you don't have current work, you aren't ready to be represented by a gallery.

Have your Biography and your Artist Statement either printed out or on your website. These things are important to some galleries. If you aren't sure how to write your Biography or Artist Statement, there are online guides that you can follow and many books written on the subject. A good book that will help with this is titled *Art-Write: The Writing Guide for Visual Artists* by Vicki Krohn Amerose. Another excellent resource is Alyson Stanfield's book, *I'd Rather be in the Studio*.

If you have won awards for your art, or have been written about in the media, have those items clearly shown on your website as well. If you don't have a website, then do it the old fashioned way and have printouts in a neat booklet.

Getting into a good gallery is easier if you have developed relationships in the art community or your work has already been selling very well. The gallery has to be sure that your work will sell before they commit wall space to your art. Galleries are essentially a retail store; they lose money every day that something on the wall doesn't sell.

The best way to get into a gallery is to form relationships with people at galleries and in your local art community. You do this by volunteering, joining art associations and befriending other artists.

Attend gallery shows and meet the people who work there. Don't discuss your art at another artist's show, as that is poor form. Instead, use that time to get to know the gallery representatives and their exhibiting artists on a personal level. Once you've met someone in person, they will be more likely to warm up to you.

Relationship building takes time so begin today; get out and join associations, attend exhibits and form new friendships. One of the top galleries in Laguna Beach, CA recently invited Drew to do a solo exhibit. We were overjoyed. It is to date the finest gallery Drew has ever be invited to exhibit in. This opportunity came about because we have become friends with the owners; we have mutual friends and run into them at parties often. One evening we attended one of their gallery shows. It was that night that the owner came up with the idea. He said, "let's do a show with Drew."

The second best way to get into a gallery is by introduction from someone who knows you and knows the decision maker at the gallery. Being introduced is a guarantee to at least get a meeting to show your work.

The least recommended way to get into a gallery is to do what most artists do, which is to cold-call and ask for an appointment with someone they've never formed a relationship with. You can do this, but don't feel bad if it takes many attempts to get a response. Most galleries are so inundated with artists submitting work to them that they can't respond to all inquiries. Your emails or calls may go unanswered.

When you send an email, remember to include your full name and contact information and links to your website and social media sites. I get emails from artists all the time, asking me to look at their work, and then they don't even include links to where I can find it! Make it easy on the person who gets your email. If they have to work too hard to find out more about you and your work, they will hit "delete."

If a gallery doesn't accept your work for any reason at all, respond gracefully. Never take it personally. Ask them to give you feedback so that you can make improvements to your presentation. Thank them for their time and tell them to let you know if anything changes in the future. Always keep the door open, as what isn't a fit for them today may be a fit for them next year. Don't allow yourself to get angry or bitter. You will have to go through a lot of "nos" to get to a "yes."

CONSIGNMENT AGREEMENT

After being accepted into a gallery, the next step is to discuss the details. Ask questions such as: What is the gallery's commission? Who pays for the art to be shipped to the gallery? Who pays for the art to be returned, if it doesn't sell? How many days after a piece sells will you be paid?

Next, determine which of your pieces will go into the gallery. This would be decided by you and/or the gallery representative. Before delivering the work, have a consignment agreement signed by both you and the gallery that includes details. Below are a few examples of important points to include in the agreement:

- How much you will be paid (usually in a %)
- When will you be paid (i.e. on the fifteenth of each month for sales made the previous month)
- Who pays for shipping to and from the gallery (i.e. artist pays to ship items to the gallery, gallery pays to return unsold items)
- The gallery is required to insure the artwork while in its possession
- A list of each art piece, size, medium and artist's required retail price

Now for a little out of the box thinking: ask the gallery to provide you with the collector's name and contact information. We require this of all of our galleries, as we have kept a detailed list of all of Drew's buyers going back to 1998. Knowing who owns each original is an important historical record. Just this year, our list has come in handy, as we prepare for a museum exhibit of Drew's work. The museum has asked us for the names of the buyers of some of Drew's most iconic pieces so that they can obtain them on loan for the exhibit. If we hadn't been diligent with collecting this information, we wouldn't know who the owners are.

Some galleries will refuse to provide you with this information, others will oblige. It doesn't hurt to ask. You could include a statement in your consignment agreement that reads as follows:

"The Gallery will provide Artist with the buyer(s) of any original Artwork(s) contact information including: name, address, phone number and email address at the time of payment to the Artist."

When deducting the high cost of materials from the gallery/artist split, such as the example I gave earlier when using a high priced surfboard instead of a canvas, you could include a statement in the consignment agreement that reads similar to this (of course, change the wording as necessary):

"The Gallery and the Artist agree that the Gallery's commission is to be 50% of the Retail Price of the Original Artwork, except for the sale of art on _____, in which case, the Gallery's commission is to be 50% of the Retail Price of the Original Artwork after $1,000 is deducted from the sale price. (i.e. art piece sells for $5,000; the 50% commission is determined in this manner: $5,000 sale price minus $1,000 material expenses = $4,000 x 50% = $2,000 total payable to The Gallery.)"

You can access a template for a consignment agreement through through my website at www.mariabrophy.com.

RED FLAGS

Watch out for red flags in any contract and don't be afraid to ask for changes to it. Every agreement is negotiable. If a gallery gives you a consignment agreement that has anything in it that you don't want, ask them to change it. A good business relationship is one that works well for both parties. A good gallery will respect your wishes and work with you on the language.

Watch out for these warning signs when going into an agreement with a gallery:

REFUSES TO SIGN A CONSIGNMENT AGREEMENT

Beware of the gallery representative that won't sign a consignment agreement. You must have it in writing that they are in possession of your artwork and that it is on consignment. The consignment agreement protects you from loss of art due to theft, natural disaster and bankruptcy. It also details how much and when you will be paid.

When the economy crashed in 2008 and galleries went out of business, many artists lost their artworks. The bankruptcy courts seized all assets of the bankrupt galleries, including prints, paintings and sculptures. Without proof that the artist owned the works, they could not get the art returned to them. A consignment agreement protects against this.

I've had gallery owners tell me, "I don't sign agreements. I work with a hand shake." I pretend not to hear it, and then bring them an agreement to sign. I've been able to get every single one signed to date. If someone doesn't want to sign an agreement, ask them why. Remind them that it protects both parties, and let them know that you'll be bringing them an agreement to sign. Don't take no for an answer. Most likely, they will sign it for you. If they refuse, don't leave your art in their possession.

EXCLUSIVE

Exclusive means that you agree not to sell art in any other gallery in the area specified. Don't agree to a worldwide, statewide or even county-wide exclusive with a gallery. If you agree to an exclusive, it should only be in the immediate geographical area in which the gallery is located.

Many galleries don't want to compete with other galleries to sell your work, and that is completely understandable. However, it will harm your earning potential if you agree to a broad exclusive agreement. Having your art in other galleries elsewhere in the world actually benefits the gallery. The more your work is seen and known, the better it will sell for everyone.

I once had a gallery try to get me to sign an agreement that gave them worldwide exclusivity! That meant that we couldn't show Drew's work in any other gallery in the world, which was entirely unreasonable. I convinced the owner to change it to read that it was exclusive to Corona Del Mar, California, which is where they were located. This gave him what he wanted, which was no local competition.

If you're in a big city, like New York, the agreement might read "Exclusive to the Chelsea District." If you're in Los Angeles, it might read "Exclusive to Sunset Blvd in Hollywood." If you're in a small town, it might read "Exclusive to Haliewa, Hawaii."

NOT WILLING TO PAY SHIPPING ONE WAY

Typically the artist pays to ship the art to the gallery. Most galleries will agree to pay for shipping to return any unsold work back to the artist. It is reasonable and fair for a gallery to share in this responsibility.

OVERSEAS GALLERIES

Be careful when sending artwork overseas. Once it's gone, it is gone forever, and getting art back will be nearly impossible if the people you are dealing with are not reputable. I once had an entire shipment of artwork go to France. It took me three years to get just part of it back and I was not paid for the rest. An alternative is to have the overseas gallery pay you a deposit in advance of what they will make if they sell your work. If the work doesn't sell, you can return their money when you get it back unharmed.

PAY TO PLAY

Beware of galleries that charge you an excessive fee to be shown in their gallery. These are referred to as "vanity galleries" and they are known for taking money from artists who are desperate to show their work.

A vanity gallery makes its money off of the artist, not off of selling artwork. This business model removes all motivation for the gallery to sell art. The gallery wins, the artist loses.

Vanity galleries target artists who do not have a strong following yet. They will send a letter writing flattering words that pulls the artist into their program. Unfortunately, some artists fall for it and spend a lot of money to be "represented" by a gallery who isn't truly interested in selling their work.

The fees that vanity galleries charge can be excessive. I know of artists who have fallen prey and have paid tens of thousands of dollars, with the promise that they would make their money back in art sales. But the promises were not kept.

Vanity galleries will accept any artist at any level, as long as they can pay. If you exhibit at a vanity gallery, don't put it on your website or resume, as it will be a red flag to any reputable gallery that considers you. It harms you more than helps you.

A better option is to apply to juried shows and exhibits. You can find them through online websites such as www. callforentry.org and www.callforentries.com.

RENT A WALL

Some galleries will rent wall space to artists. This helps the gallery cover their overhead costs. This arrangement is a hybrid between the traditional gallery and the vanity gallery. The deals often work like this; the gallery charges the artist a monthly rental fee for wall space (i.e. $250/month) and then when an art piece sells, the artist keeps 80% and the gallery keeps 20%. The deals vary from gallery to gallery, but this is the basic idea.

Many reputable galleries are doing this now, but there are some bad ones out there, too. If you are considering renting gallery wall space, do your homework first. Call at least three other artists who have been renting space from the gallery and ask if the gallery is paying the artists on time and if they have kept their promises. Also, be sure to have a consignment agreement in place.

16

YOUR NETWORK = YOUR NET WORTH

"If you need a cash flow infusion in your business, reach out to ten previous clients"
—Tiffany Peterson, Success Coach

Many creative entrepreneurs make the mistake of putting all of their marketing efforts into getting new clients, while ignoring the clients who have already bought from them.

It is a fact that your past buyers will buy from you again and again. This is because if they bought from you once, they are a qualified buyer.

It is your responsibility to keep in touch, not theirs. Many think that if a client was happy with their purchase, they will come back for more. But that's not what happens. People get busy, they lose your contact information, or they just plain forget as their day-to-day lives take over.

SELLING ART IS A LONG-TERM GAME

Selling art isn't like selling candles; the candle runs out and the buyer needs a new one. Artwork is often bought when one buys a new home, sets up a new office, or redecorates. These events are spread out over years.

This means that your clients may only purchase art once every few years. When they are ready to buy a new piece, you want to be the first artist they think of.

WHY YOUR CLIENTS WILL CONTINUE TO BUY FROM YOU, AGAIN AND AGAIN

Finding new buyers is hard work. How many times have you had potential clients ask for a price quote or inquire about your work, yet end up not buying? It's because they weren't a qualified buyer.

The people who have bought from you before are already qualified. You have already connected with them. You have already done the hardest thing of all—to win them as a client! They will buy from you again because they have the funds, they love your work, and because you were an absolute dream to do business with… right?

It is much easier to sell to someone who has bought from you in the past, than to sell to a complete stranger. This is because people are run by their habits; they tend to shop in the same places for the same things over and over again. Also, people like to buy from people they know.

To sell again and again to your past clients, you have to stay in constant contact with them. Why do you think Coke is still advertising? Everyone knows what Coke is. They know if they like it or not. But if Coke stopped connecting with the public, they would eventually be forgotten. This logic applies to artists, too.

HOW TO NOURISH YOUR NETWORK

To effectively nourish your network, implement a reminder system that is consistent and long term. It is a known standard in sales that people have to see a message at least seven times before they buy. To get results, you have to be consistent. Below are a few ways to do this:

- Newsletters
- Handwritten Notes
- Postcard mailers
- Phone calls
- Holiday cards
- In Person Meetings over coffee, a hike, a golfing session, etc.

Choose two or three methods that work best for you. I will detail a few below.

NEWSLETTERS BY EMAIL

This is a very powerful way to continually connect with your network. It's results-driven because:

1. A newsletter allows you to update your clients on new art or projects.
2. It keeps you in the forefront of their minds.
3. They watch you grow as an artist over time, and will begin to feel as though they know you well.
4. They become a part of your story.

Many artists begin a newsletter program only to abandon it later, because it can be a lot of work. But it doesn't have to be hard. To make it easier, keep your newsletters very simple. It could be one image with a short description, and then a call to action.

A call to action tells the reader what you want them to do, such as "call me if you want to commission a piece" or "click here to buy this print."

Maria Scrivan, a cartoonist that I've had the pleasure of working with, sends a weekly newsletter titled "Cartoon of the Week." It's very simple; every week she sends an email that has one photo of a recent cartoon, a short description about it, and a call to action such as "to license my cartoons, contact me."

Any artist can use a simple email newsletter format – that is, to have each newsletter feature one art piece, write a description of the art, and include a "call to action". Be sure to have the "call to action" include a link that leads to a sales page on your website or online store.

Fine artist Paula Jones sends a monthly newsletter to her email list. Her newsletters are long and in them she writes in great depth. She uses a consistent format; she features a new piece of art and shares a deep thought that she is pondering.

Find a consistent format that works for you. Keep it simple if you are short on time. Send your newsletter at the same time every week or month and continue to add names to your email list.

POSTCARD MAILERS

About ten years ago, when we sold art directly to retailers, we instituted a postcard campaign. Every 2 months we mailed a postcard to over 500 boutiques. Each postcard had just one image on it; the latest painting by Drew Brophy. The other side of the card had a "call to action" encouraging them to place an order for art prints.

After six months of mailing these postcards, I started to see powerful results. Sales increased significantly. People told me that they were "collecting" the postcards. Many hung them on their walls behind their store counters.

Postcards can be a powerful tool, provided that:

1. You are consistent. Commit to mailing a postcard every one or two months for at least a year.
2. Show just ONE piece of art on the front of the postcard (not a hodge-podge of multiple images, as it won't get the attention it deserves).

3. Have a "call to action" on the back with all of your contact info.
4. Mail them in envelopes. Otherwise, they will get beat up by the post office and will not make the best impression when received.

MAIL HANDWRITTEN NOTES

Most of us don't mail hand-written notes to people anymore. That's why it's so memorable when you do it. Here's a few ideas on when to send notes:

1. When an art piece sells: Send a handwritten thank you note to every person that buys an art piece from you; mail it one week after delivery.
2. Weekly: Set up a system where you mail a handwritten note to five of your past clients weekly. Let them know you are thinking of them. You can even send them an article or something that may be of interest to them.
3. Yearly: Send a handwritten note to your clients during the Holidays. This is an easy thing to remember – make it a yearly practice.

CONNECT IN PERSON

Take your clients to coffee, on a hike, or golfing; whatever fits your personality. These are bonding events that turn clients into friends.

One of our clients is a reggae band called SOWFLO from Florida. One week they were touring California so we invited them to go surfing with us. A bus of seven Rastafarian-looking guys pulled up to our studio. We had an amazing day of surfing, standup paddling and sunshine. It made me love my job even more!

PHONE CALLS

If you called five people every day, you would see a massive increase in art sales. Calling past buyers and newly interested buyers reminds them that you are available and maintains the relationship.

Once I called on a previous client in the advertising world that we hadn't talked to in two years. He said it was great that I called because he had a project that Drew would be perfect for. He hired Drew for an illustration project on the spot.

When making phone calls, don't do so with the intention of selling. Instead, call with the genuine intention to ask how they are doing and if there's anything you can help them with. Be interested in their lives and what's going on. The purpose of the call is to nourish the relationship. If a sale comes from it, that's a bonus.

Relationships are like flowers; they must be watered or they will die. Sometimes I get so busy with tending to our business, a household and two kids, there isn't time for anything else. I can easily forget to nourish my network.

And that's where systems and habits come into play.

To help stay on track, I have put systems into place for Drew Brophy Art Collectors. My online calendar is filled with reminders to help me remember.

Below is an example of a system we follow when an original piece of art sells to a collector:

- The artwork is shipped
- After delivery, a personal phone call is made to the collector to make sure it arrived safely
- One week later, a hand-written thank you card is mailed
- With permission, their email is added to our newsletter list
- They are added to our VIP Collectors list, which means they get special offers before anyone else on new artworks
- As a VIP, they receive holiday greeting cards and special invites to events

HOW WILL YOU NOURISH YOUR NETWORK?

Put a system in place today. Use the Nourish Your Network Worksheet on the next page.

Take a few minutes to answer the questions right now. The intention is to get you thinking of systems that you can implement today, which will help you to consistently nourish your collectors.

NOURISH MY NETWORK WORKSHEET

Your Network = Your Net Worth! $$$

INSTRUCTIONS: Brainstorm how you will nourish your network of clients.

How will I show appreciation and re-connect with my clients for the next 4 quarters (one year)? (i.e. Postcard mailers, handwritten notes, Holiday cards, phone calls, a lunch, email list).

Quarter 1:

Quarter 2:

Quarter 3:

Quarter 4:

THE TOP FIVE CLIENTS/COLLECTORS WHO MADE PURCHASES FROM ME IN THE PAST:

1.
2.
3.

4.

5.

HOW will I show extra appreciation to my top clients listed above?

WHO will I call TODAY to re-connect with? (Not to sell, but to say "hello"). List at least 5 names:

1.

2.

3.

4.

5.

17

SELF PROMOTION STRATEGIES

Self-Promotion has gotten a bad rap. Many complain, "I don't wanna go around talking about myself." But if you look at all of the people who have created success without the backing of a big company or a trust fund left by a wealthy uncle, you'll find that self-promotion was a necessary piece of the puzzle.

When Drew was in his twenties, he had no one to rely on but himself. Survival meant getting new art commissions, which required self promotion.

He had a habit that drove his surfer buddies crazy; he would carry his art portfolio with him everywhere he went. When they would go to a beach party, Drew would arrive with a six-pack of beer under one arm and his giant, black portfolio book under the other.

Inevitably, amongst the loud music and youthful debauchery, a small crowd of people would gather around Drew as he flipped the pages of his big black book, admiring his art and asking to see more.

Even though Drew's life as an artist was the envy of his nine-to-fiver friends, they taunted him, calling him "Promo Drew." Drew would defend himself, saying, "Hey, if I don't promote myself, who will?"

His self-promotion got results. Most of Drew's art commissions at that pre-internet age came from meeting people, in person, and telling them about his art. The reality is that no one is going promote your work for you; you have to do it yourself.

There are countless ways to promote your work. You don't have to do everything all at once, now. It's best to choose one method to implement at a time. Learn how to do it well, spend time on it, and once you feel you can do it in your sleep, then add another promotional tool, and repeat.

Consistency is key. If you decide that making videos is a good place to start, make a dozen or more. The best thing to do is make a video regularly, for example, once a week, for a year. Over time you'll gain a viewership, and you'll eventually see the marketing value of it.

You have to be patient, because the value of promotion doesn't show up right away. It takes time, consistency, and tenacity to see results.

NETWORKING LIVE

Your best results will come from promoting yourself, live, in person. People like people they meet. You become known to them. They are more likely to choose you for that event or exhibit over someone they haven't met.

The more people you meet, the greater chance you have of making connections that lead you to new collectors. To meet more people, you have to get out and network at live events or meetings. While you're there, make it a habit to meet as many new people as you can. **Set a goal to introduce yourself and talk to a minimum of ten people at each event.** When you meet people, introduce yourself as an artist. This is the simplest and most effective form of promotion.

FOR THE INTROVERT

If you feel awkward in social situations I have two terrific tools for you that will be a game changer if you get in the habit of using them. And if you're an extrovert, these tools will take your game to the next level.

Social Networking Tool #1: Decide who you want to meet

Before attending an event, decide WHO you will meet there. Examples of people you might want to meet would be:

- A gallery owner that you've been trying to get a meeting with.
- An art collector.
- Influential art dealer or broker.
- Your area's best interior designer.
- An artist that you admire.
- Licensing manager of a large company you wish to work with.
- Anyone you want to connect with personally.

Write a list of the names of at least three people you wish to meet at the event. If you don't know names, then write down the types of people. Writing it down using a pen on paper makes it more likely that your subconscious will recognize the opportunity to meet those people and then act on it. Slip this paper in your pocket and take it with you, so you can remind yourself of your intention.

Social Networking Tool #2: Visualize your Connection

This next tool is true magic, and if your mind is open enough to do it, you will get such powerful results that you will wonder why no one else is talking about it!

Before attending any event, take ten minutes to mentally design the interactions you wish to have with people. First, decide who you want to meet (Tool #1).

Next, decide how you want to interact with each person. Close your eyes and take a few minutes to visualize in your mind how you will feel when talking to them. Then visualize how you will make them feel talking to you. Examples of feelings that you may choose could be funny, joyful, inspired, appreciated, peaceful, etc. Place an emphasis on how you will give to them in the conversation; for example, you will give them acceptance, understanding, love, or joy. Make sure it comes from your heart and from a place of selflessness. Visualize yourself enjoying being there and truly connecting with each person that you intend to connect with. This next step is very important: while visualizing, feel the feelings that you want to have while connecting with each person. Do this exercise right before going to the event. It's highly effective.

Last summer Drew was exhibiting in a group art show. We were told that one very influential Los Angeles art collector would be there. I decided to meet him and connect with him on a personal level. I scoured his social media sites to get to know him a little better. And then, before the event, I took the time to visualize myself talking and laughing with him. It was my intention to make this person feel appreciated, loved and fun while in my presence. Later that night at the exhibit, I walked up to him and introduced myself. I commented on something funny that he had posted on Facebook and then we had a great laugh together. Just as I imagined in my visualization, we connected deeply. Since then, we have talked numerous times and have formed a good relationship.

NETWORKING = RELATIONSHIPS = BUSINESS GROWTH

Relationships are built over time and require "watering" to stay alive. Imagine promoting your work as if you are planting seeds. Some will blossom right away, some will take longer to grow.

Sprinkle seeds of business everywhere you go. Make sure that every single person you meet knows what you're passionate about and what you're selling. Don't shove it down their throats, but casually drop it into conversation, planting seeds in the minds of people you meet. If someone shows interest and starts asking you questions, then you can tell them more.

It's not uncommon for someone to call me with a commission a year after I met them. In the art business, timing is everything. If the person you meet isn't ready for your art now, they may be sometime in the future.

GENERATING CONFIDENCE
IN SOCIAL SITUATIONS

No one is born with confidence. Confidence is generated from inside yourself. You can learn to generate your own inner confidence with practice.

If meeting people is difficult for you, have faith that it will get easier with practice. There are techniques that you can learn to help you feel confident in social situations.

I often feel awkward in social situations. My friends would laugh at that and tell me that I look perfectly comfortable socially. But I disagree. Inside, sometimes I feel out of place. **But there is no room for shyness in business.** I've always known that if I want to get ahead in life, I have to become more outgoing. I've been training myself to learn how to talk to people socially for years.

If there is only one thing you do to make yourself a better connector of people, it should be this: make every person you meet feel as though they are important.

The best lesson I ever learned about how to talk to people was from actor Jerry O'Connell in a San Clemente sushi restaurant one night many years ago. I was having dinner with Jerry, Drew, and another actor named Ted Detwiler, who is one of Drew's childhood friends. Drew and Ted were in a deep conversation about surfing at the other end of the table. Jerry was seated directly across from me. I don't remember what we talked about, but I'll never forget how he made me feel. The entire time we talked, he was leaning over the table, looking in my eyes and listening intently to every word I said, with a warmness about him that said "I hear you, I accept you." He gave me his undivided attention. He made me feel as though I was the most interesting person he's ever met.

Below are ten techniques that will help you to easily talk to people:

1. Zero in on one person at a time to talk to. If you see someone standing alone at an event, confidently put your hand out and say "Hi, I'm Maria. What's your name?" After they answer, then ask an open-ended question such as, "What brings you here tonight?" This is a great conversation opener. And the best part about approaching someone who is alone is that you are doing them a great favor. They probably were wishing they had someone to talk to.

2. Look them in the eye. Be laser-focused on their face and their words, as if they are the only person in the room. Repeat their name back to them, "Hi Blake, so good to meet you." Remember their name. Honor the person that they are. Don't look around at others in the room. Don't look at your watch or phone. Be respectful of their brief time with you. Give warmth. Give a hug if

it's appropriate. Some of the best business meetings I've ever had ended with a hug.

3. Know that all people are the same. Janitors, presidents, and everyone in between. We all have the desire to be loved and noticed. We love our families. We love our pets. We love to eat. There are more similarities between people than there are differences. Once you believe this, it's easier to connect with others.

4. Focus on the other person, not yourself. One of the reasons we feel insecure or uncomfortable is because we are too busy thinking about how we look to others. If you focus on the person you are talking to, you can't focus on yourself. This is what saves you.

5. Ask open-ended questions, such as "where are you from", "what do you like about this event", or "what brought you here". And then listen. Care about the person and what they have to say.

6. Look for hooks that you can connect with. If they say "I came tonight because Julie told me I'd like it" and you know Julie, say "Oh, Julie and I have been friends since college. How did you two meet?"

7. Look for things you love about the person as they speak to you. Yes, even with strangers. This is powerfully effective! Feel love when you are admiring them as they talk. Give genuine compliments.

When we focus on what we love about someone, we put out friendly, loving vibrations. People feel your vibrations and react to it like a mirror. They give you love back and they don't even realize it. This is one technique that I've used again and again, especially in business meetings where I'm nervous. It helps me to remove my nervousness and focus on the wonderful aspects of the person I'm with.

8. Never judge someone by the way they look. Be kind to everyone. Sometimes the most important person in the room is the most subtle and the least important is the best dressed.

   One day a bare-footed, disheveled looking man walked into our studio. He looked more like a beggar than a buyer. He asked me to show him Drew's paintings, so I begrudgingly showed him around, annoyed that he was taking me away from my work. Then he surprised me by purchasing two paintings, totaling $8,000, which he paid for right then and there. I learned not to judge people after that.

9. Dress your best, whatever that means to you. Our clothing and hair and makeup can either make us feel confident or insecure. Wear what makes you feel confident.

10. Have fun. When you're smiling and laughing and not taking life too seriously, you feel more confident and are attractive to others.

Find a way to get yourself in a fun, joyous mood before you go to any event. Listen to loud music, pet your dog, chant your oms or laugh a lot in the car on the ride there.

SELF PROMOTION STRATEGIES

Below is a list of Self-Promotion and Marketing strategies that you can implement right now:

Never leave home without your business cards. Your card should have an example of your art on the front and your complete contact information on the back, including your phone number, email address and a website where they can view your work.

Whenever you meet someone new, tell them you're an artist and hand them a business card. Ask them to let you know if there's anything you can do for them in the future.

Auto Wrap or paint your vehicle with your artwork. Drew painted our big Ford van all the way around with a beautiful surf inspired mural. On each side of the van, we have attached weather-proof business card holders.

Get out of your comfort zone and meet new people. Join art associations and clubs. Join the local Chamber of Commerce. Go to events or functions where you are most likely to meet your right buyer.

Go directly to clients, galleries, or businesses that you want to sell to, and meet them. Don't hide behind emails and social media.

Post youtube.com videos of you creating. This is very effective. People want to buy from people they know—and if they watch you on a video, they feel like they know you. To get results, this method requires consistent video postings over a long period of time and a second method of getting the videos out to people, either by newsletters or other social media channels. *Caution: If you make "how to" videos, you will attract artists, not art buyers. When creating the videos, be sure that the language you use and the subject matter you shoot is designed to speak directly to your right buyer, not to other artists.

Send newsletters. Most of our art sales come from newsletter mailings. Build up a list of friends, family and fans and, with their permission, send them a bi-monthly newsletter with news of what you're working on.

Send a press release to the media when you have something to announce, like a new exhibit, an open house or a new series that you are creating. Learn how to properly write press releases so that the media wants to pick up your story. There are many books and blog posts on how to do this.

Teach a class. Give something of value to your local community, share your knowledge, and gain a few new customers. If you are a webmaster, give a two hour class on SEO or how to set up a website. If you're an artist, give art classes or hold a "wine and paint" class. Share your expertise, and you'll become known as the expert in your field.

Volunteer at a networking event, trade show or business gathering. This is an easy and fun way to meet influential people in your area. If you volunteer to help at an event, you'll inevitably meet everyone there. Help clean up after the event, and most likely you'll be rubbing elbows with the most important people, because the leaders are the ones making events happen and often they're the last ones to leave.

Join a Meet-Up Group that shares your same interests. Go to www.meetup.com, type in something you're interested in (i.e. "photography" or "ceramics" or "writing") and your zip code, and you'll find many options. This will expose you to people that can lead you to opportunities.

Facebook, Twitter, Instagram, Pinterest and Google+ are just a few of many social sites that artists are using to post their artwork and reach people online. Elsewhere in this book we lightly cover social media. For up-to-date details on how to set up and run your social media accounts, do an online search to find one of many articles that will help.

Let's do a little brainstorming on promoting your work. Get your notebook and a pen, and write the answers to the following questions:

1. List five People who have bought from you in the past. Then list how they found you and your work.
2. List five people or companies that you would like to do business with. Then write down places where you can meet these people.
3. List five live events or function that you can attend. Then write down the dates that you will attend them. Put these dates on your calendar and commit to them.

18

ART LICENSING

Many artists dream of seeing their artwork printed on products and placed on store shelves. Imagine walking into a Nordstrom and seeing your art printed on silk scarves or men's neckties. That would feel great, wouldn't it? To make this happen, you either have to build your own manufacturing business, get investors, and spend years building up sales with retailers, or, you can license your art to a manufacturer and let them do all the work.

Licensing is a much easier way! When you license your art to a manufacturer, they are responsible to make, market and sell the products that your artwork is printed on. Your responsibility is to provide the artwork. In return, you are paid either a flat fee or a royalty.

A few years before I left my corporate job, I worked part time managing Drew's art business. We were selling Drew's art prints to retailers and original painting commissions to collectors. The retailers were placing $300 print orders. Each order required the time to mat and bag the prints, then ship them, then bill the customer and later make collection calls. The profit margins were good, but we had to sell to hundreds of stores to make a good living from it. We hired two full time employees to help. The employees required managing from us as well. We learned quickly that this business model took a lot of energy and effort to generate the kind of money we wanted to earn.

Though we were selling a lot of art, we had become hamsters on a treadmill. The more successful we became, the more behind we got. During busy months, in addition to orders from retailers, I would have many commissioned projects for Drew and the cash would flow in. But, Drew would have to bust his butt to churn out the work. Sometimes he would work seven days a week for long hours just to keep up with the demand.

While having a plethora of commissioned projects is a dream for many artists, it's a tough spot to be in, because creating art then becomes like digging ditches. You are only paid once, for each ditch that you dig. You take that money and pay your mortgage and feed your kids, and then the money is gone, and now you need to dig more ditches. Digging ditches 24-7 is exhausting work, even if you love it.

While Drew is extremely efficient, the constant "digging ditches" became a never ending cycle of exhaustion and burn out. We realized that we would have to leverage his artwork so that we could make money off of an image more than one time.

This way, for every "ditch" that he digs, we will be paid for it not just once, but many times for years to come.

It was in 2001 when we had our "aha" moment about licensing art. We had closed a deal with Wham-O, one of the largest toy manufacturers in the U.S. We licensed a line of Drew's wild surf and fish art for their kid's boogie boards. We had a friend who worked at the company, Petie, who helped make the deal happen for us.

Wham O boogie boards was our first official art licensing deal and it was what gave us the idea that we could utilize Drew's large library of artwork for thousands of products. At the time, licensing only made up about 10% of our income. We decided that year that we would make it our focus to increase our licensing to 60% of our income.

The artwork we provided Wham-O was a combination of existing artworks and new illustrations. Drew creates art old-school illustration style. Everything he creates is an actual painting, which we get a high res scan of. When licensing, you only have to provide your client with the digital images. So we kept the original paintings and sold them to collectors, which earned us more money. We also licensed the images to other companies for non-competing products, such as t-shirts and stickers. We were making money from the same art over and over again.

We had a few artists ask if we felt that it would hurt Drew's brand, putting his art on boogie boards. We had worried about that initially. Later, we found that instead of hurting Drew's brand, it enhanced it. One of Drew's goals is to bring joy to people with his art. Seeing kids happily playing with his boogie boards on the beach is evidence that we have reached that goal. Bringing joy to people can never hurt your brand!

Our deal with Wham-O went huge; they sold hundreds of thousands of Drew Brophy boogie boards each year, all over the world. In 2006 Drew took a surf trip to South Africa and was excited to see kids on the beach near J-Bay playing with his boogie boards. The Brophy boogie boards were everywhere, and each one bore Drew's art, signature and name.

We continued our license with Wham-O for many years, giving them new artwork to freshen up the line every year or two. Our deal ended seven years later, after Wham-O was sold to a Chinese company.

The best thing about our deal with Wham-O, and other licensing deals with large companies, is that we are paid licensing fees while at the same time, Drew's name and art is being marketed on a level that we could never do ourselves. It's definitely a great way to work smarter, not harder.

LICENSING AS A BUSINESS MODEL

Licensing your art is a business model that generates an additional stream of income, allowing you to earn money off of your images again and again.

Licensing means that the artist (the Licensor) grants another entity (the Licensee) the rights to use the artwork for a temporary period of time for a specific usage. Some people would describe licensing as "renting" images to a manufacturer to print on their products. As the owner of the artwork, you continue to keep ownership of your copyrights to the artwork while it's licensed, and, you can choose to do anything you want with the artwork, as long as your contract doesn't restrict it.

An example of art licensing is an artist who creates a line of Elvis themed images and gives temporary rights to a manufacturer to print those images on clothing, ceramics and music boxes, and then sell them to gift stores. The manufacturer benefits by having art that will make their products sell well, and the artist benefits by being paid for it.

A very simple example of licensing, one that many artists are already doing and don't even realize it, is when an artist creates a t-shirt design for a company and allows that company to print and sell the t-shirts.

Before our first official art licensing deal with Wham-O, Drew had been unofficially licensing his art to the surf company, Lost Surfboards. For many years, Drew's art adorned Lost's surfboards, wallets, clothing, and stickers. Since both Drew and Lost were inexperienced with licensing in those days, they didn't have a formal contract. Instead, Drew would hand-write on his invoices what the usage rights were. Drew created thousands of images for Lost over the course of many years and he owns the copyrights to every image.

After Drew's surf trip to South Africa, he was inspired to paint *Sunrise*, a painting that has since become wildly popular. So popular, in fact, that it is one of the most copied artworks in surf. The original painting was painted on a large canvas and sold quickly in a Corona del Mar, CA gallery. Since then, we have licensed *Sunrise* to many different companies. It's been licensed to a skateboard company, a wall-art company, a glassware company, a cell phone cover company and many others. All of those companies paid us a royalty to use the artwork on their products. Since each agreement limited their use to their specific product, we licensed the art to other companies for non-competing products. At the same time, we continue to sell paper and canvas reproductions of *Sunrise* to our own collectors through drewbrophy.com store and in our gallery. To date, we have earned over a quarter of a million dollars in royalties just from *Sunrise*. Just think, if we had sold the original painting and all of its rights away, we would have earned only a fraction of that amount.

Many artists will ask me how much money they can make by licensing their art. It depends. Some artists, the very rare, super successful ones, earn over a million a year in royalties. Some artists will sign license deals and never see a dime. And some artists have made it their full time job.

The amount of money you can make in licensing depends on three things:

1. How well your art applies to commercial products
2. How popular your images are (or can be), and
3. How much time you are willing to put into the business of licensing

THE LICENSING CONTRACT

The agreement you have with a licensee will determine how much money you make and what they are allowed to do with the artwork, and what you are allowed to do with it, while the license is in effect.

Every agreement is different and depends on the details of what the licensee will be doing with the art, such as: How many products will they print the art on; how many images do they want; where will they be sold; what are the sales projections; what is the retail price; will they use existing art or require you to create new art? These questions should be answered in the first few conversations you have with your licensee, before agreeing to a price or royalty.

In a typical agreement, the artist grants rights to their licensee to use the art for a temporary period of time (i.e. 2 years), in a specific geographical territory (i.e. the United States), for a specific usage (i.e. silk scarves, ladies hats and handbags). While an image is being licensed, the artist can continue to create and sell other products with the artwork, as long as their agreement doesn't restrict it. All of these details, and more, should be included in a written agreement.

Most companies will want to use their own licensing contract. In that case, please have an attorney that specializes in licensing help you with it. It's important to be aware of contract language that can harm your future earning potential.

If you plan on regularly licensing your artwork, it's best to invest in having an attorney create a license agreement for you that you can use again and again. I also have a license agreement template that you can use. You can find it at www.mariabrophy.com.

Remember, every agreement is negotiable. If the contract has language that you don't want to agree to, ask them to change it. You don't have to agree to anything you don't want to.

MORE TO KNOW ABOUT LICENSING

Anyone can license their art if they own the copyrights, including cartoonists, digital artists, painters, sculptors, photographers and writers. In addition to licensing artwork, if you're a well-known personality or athlete, you can license your name and likeness. Snowboarder Sean White has an entire line of boy's clothing for sale in Target under his own name.

Often I'm asked if abstract art can be licensed. The answer is, sometimes. Abstracts typically don't work well with commercial products, however, there are always exceptions. I've seen beautiful abstract art printed on ladies silk scarves and luxury items. Also, licensing isn't just about products, it also applies to wall art. Most abstracts will do well with wall art.

Traditional licensing is when you license your work to a manufacturer and they sell your commercial products in mass market or mainstream retailers. This is what many artists aspire to do. But, traditional licensing tends to pay less, and to earn a good living from it you must have dozens of active licenses and your artwork must have a very strong commercial appeal and be up to date on recent trends.

Sadly, in traditional licensing there is a large number of artists vying for the deals, and in their desperation, they have lowered their own value. Artists that are not business-educated, or that are desperate, will agree to bad license deals that pay nothing up front and very little in royalties. I have seen contracts that offer the artist zero up front advance with a 2% royalty and no guarantees.

Artists who agree to bad deals have ruined it for the professional artists who are trying to make a living, because now manufacturers are trained to not respect the artist. They say "well, if you refuse to license at these rates, there are a hundred other artists who will do it for nearly nothing." And so it is.

Non-traditional art licensing is where the money is. I consider non-traditional licensing to be when you license your work for advertising campaigns or a company's branding or for boutique retailers or for a niche market or any other usage that doesn't fall under traditional licensing. You'll earn more because so few artists are making their work available in this way and they haven't screwed up the market value yet. I've been able to consistently get anywhere from $6,000 to $30,000 advance payments in these markets, where in traditional licensing I can barely get any advance at all.

If putting together a licensing deal takes twenty hours of work, and you'll be paid an advance of $0 with one licensee, or $6,000 with another, which would you choose? Think about this before putting too much time into a deal where there is little money up front. It takes the same amount of time to put together a good deal as it does a bad one. Choose to put your focus, time and energy into the good ones.

There is so much more to know about putting the deals together, what to charge, how to negotiate, how to find licensees, and more. If you plan on licensing your art, take the time to read everything you can find out about it. You can access a lot of free information online. You can also attend the Licensing University, put on by LIMA. And, of course, work with consultants and attorneys in the beginning to help you make the best decisions.

The most important thing to know about art licensing is that while there are rules in licensing, you don't have to follow them. You can make your own rules. If you envision your art on high quality products, you don't have to agree to low quality products. If you want to license your art to many different kinds of companies, you can. If you want to make your expensive, fine art paintings available to print on products, you can. No one can tell you what the best business model is for yourself. You get to choose.

ROYALTIES AND FLAT FEES - HOW TO PRICE LICENSING

Many years ago when Drew and I committed to growing our licensing program, I enrolled in the Licensing certificate program through LIMA's Licensing University. I was very excited to attend one of the classes titled "What to charge for licensing; Royalties and Advances."

Sitting in the front row, eager to get guidance as to what to charge, I had my notebook ready. A panel of five licensing experts sat at the front of the room, about to share their wisdom.

Pen in hand, I listened intently, waiting for the mystery to unravel. What should I charge? How much of an advance should I ask for? How much in royalty rates?

And then, one by one, each expert on the panel explained in their own words why they couldn't give us exact percentages and dollar amounts. Every single licensing deal is different.

What a disappointment! I left that class learning only one thing, and that is, even the experts have no idea how to teach newbies what to charge. I vowed at that moment to create a system for myself. Fifteen years later, it's nearly perfected, and now I can share it with you.

There are many factors to consider when it comes to working out a licensing deal. Deals can be huge, deals can be tiny. Some require a lot of work, some require no work at all. Sometimes, the deals that require the least amount of work on your end, bring you the most money. And vice-versa.

In some licensing deals, you'll be asked to create all new art; this is where a lot of work comes in. In many licensing deals, you'll only need to provide high res images of your existing art; this is less work on your end.

If you are doing a lot of work up front, you will need to make sure you get a large enough advance to cover your time.

Licensing art comes in many different forms and varied levels of complexity, such as:

1. SIMPLE: Allowing a company to use one design for a t-shirt or a single product.

2. COMPLEX: Allowing a company to use multiple images of your work for a line of products that will be sold in mass market.

3. NON-TRADITIONAL LICENSING: Allowing your work to be used for advertising campaigns, in-store point of purchase (POP) displays and online website banners.

All of these things are priced variably. Below I will give you basic guidelines based on how we charge for licensing, and you can use our pricing as a baseline to help you determine your own.

Keep in mind, if you are an artist that has a great brand recognition and is globally known, you can probably get a better deal than we do. If you are just new to the game, your deal may not be as good as ours.

In licensing, we refer to the client or manufacturer as the Licensee. You, the artist, are referred to as the Licensor.

THREE COMMON METHODS

There are three common methods of charging a Licensee for licensing your work:

1. ROYALTY: The manufacturer pays the artist a royalty percentage of their gross sales. The royalty is paid either monthly or quarterly for sales made in the previous period.

2. ROYALTY WITH ADVANCE UP FRONT: The manufacturer pays the artist a royalty percentage of their gross sales, and includes an advance payment up

front at the time of signing the contract. This advance payment is later deducted from future royalties.

3. FLAT FEE: A one-time fee is paid instead of royalties.

HOW ROYALTIES WORK

Before we get to the topic of how much to ask for, let's make sure you understand how royalties work.

Royalty payments are calculated based on the total (gross) revenues received by the Licensee for your products.

For example: You licensed your art to Perry Pickle Manufacturing for coffee mugs. They sell to a chain of stores called Racy's. You have agreed to a royalty rate of 6% with a $3,000 Advance up front.

This means that Perry Pickle Mfg is going to pay you 6% of their total gross revenues generated. Also, they agreed to pay a $3,000 Advance up front, and they paid you the advance at the time that the contract was signed.

In their first quarter, Perry Pickle Mfg received $100,000 in revenues for sales of your products.

That means that you would receive a royalty payment of $6,000.00 ($100,000 x 6% = $6,000.00), *minus* the advance of $3,000.00 up front.

The advance is "recoupable against future royalties" so your first royalty payment would be the $6,000 minus the advance amount of $3,000. Your first royalty check would be $3,000.

HOW TO DETERMINE YOUR ROYALTY % RATE

Royalty rates depend on many different factors. The top three are:

- The CATEGORY (or type) of product being produced
- The QUANTITIES expected to be sold
- The POPULARITY (STRENGTH) of the artist or brand

I'll explain each one in detail:

CATEGORY: In the licensing industry, there is one thing that is somewhat standardized, and that is the percentage of royalties that are typically paid per product category.

The royalties range from the very low end of 3% all the way up to 20%. You can access details on rates for different products in the book titled The TLL Royalty Trend Report, which is about $400 at the time of this writing. You can also find out average royalty rates by doing an online search, but the information can be hard to nail down.

The average royalty rate varies from product type to product type. Below are some of the most common categories of products and their royalty rate ranges:

Posters 8% – 18%
Greeting cards 3% - 6%
T-shirts 5% - 10%
Ceramics 3% - 8%
Cell Phone Covers 6% - 15%
Shoes 3% - 8%

The average royalty rate is a good starting point for determining what a rate should be, but as you can see above, the range is vast. You have to take into consideration the other factors shown below.

PROJECTED SALES VOLUME: The higher the projected sales volume, the lower the royalty rate will be. If the products will be sold in mass market retailers and in mass quantity, the royalty rate will be lower, because mass market retailers (like Walmart or Costco) demand better prices, which means tighter profit margins for the manufacturer.

Usually, an artist will earn more money from a lower royalty rate when products are being sold in mass market, than they would with a higher royalty rate for products being sold in small mom and pop shops. This is because instead of selling only 500 units through small stores, your licensee will be selling 50,000 units through chain stores.

The lower the projected volume, the higher the royalty should be. If the products will be sold in specialty stores and in smaller quantities, the royalty rate should be higher. Specialty stores include gift shops, boutique stores, most online stores and non-chain retailers.

For example: A t-shirt manufacturer that sells in mass market stores (Walmart, Target, chain stores) might pay 4% royalties.

A t-shirt manufacturer that sells in smaller channels such as core skateboard shops might pay 8% royalties. But, their sales numbers will be much lower than what you would see in mass market.

STRENGTH OF THE ARTIST'S BRAND: If the artist is well-known or if their art is a strong seller, the royalty rates would be on the higher end of the scale.

If the artist is unknown and new to licensing, the royalty rate might be on the lower end of the scale. In some cases, a licensee that works with many artists will have a standard royalty to offer to you. At that time, you can decide if you want to accept their offer, or negotiate for more. A licensee that isn't accustomed to working with artists will be more open to paying more.

Drew and I shy away from doing deals with manufacturers that work with a large number of artists. We have found that they tend to give the worst deals, often no advance up front and smaller percentages than what is fair. My theory on this is that they know they can get away with it, as many artists will agree to bad deals, because they don't know any better.

The best deals we've made were with companies who do not work with a large stable of artists. They are often willing to pay a healthy advance up front and a fair royalty rate. They also are more likely to sign our own contract, rather than demand that we sign theirs. I always prefer to use my own contract, because my language is already approved by me and my attorney. If I use their contract, it is a lot more work for me to read through it and make changes to it.

We've been able to get some of our licensees to pay double the standard royalty rates, because they saw the value of licensing Drew's work and knew that it would increase the sales of their products.

That said, the royalty rates that are considered standard are a good guide to use, but keep in mind, every deal is different and negotiable.

FLAT FEE METHOD OF PAYMENT

A flat fee is a lump sum that is paid up front at the time the contract is signed. There are no royalties that will be paid later.

I like flat fees when doing a deal with a very small company, because their sales volume will be low and unpredictable. I prefer the money in my hand, up front, rather than having to wait for it later.

Flat fees may be calculated either:

1. By image (i.e. $500 per image x 10 images = $5,000); or
2. In just one specified lump sum (i.e. $2,500 total).

The flat fee method is best when the licensee is either a small company that does low volume, or a startup company that does not have a track record of sales.

The disadvantage to a flat fee royalty is that if the product sells beyond expectations, you may be missing out on sharing a piece of those revenues. But that isn't really a problem, because you can protect yourself from that by giving the contract a short term, such as one year or eighteen months.

With a shorter contract, if sales are very good, the licensee will want to renew, at which time you will be paid again, or you can negotiate for a better deal.

How much of a flat fee should you ask for? Like all deals, the range is wide. I know of some artists who charge as little as $100 per image for a flat fee license. I find that to be extremely low, even if they are asking for fifty designs. It's a lot of work pulling together all of that art, even if it is already created. In the greeting card industry, an artist might be paid a flat fee of $300 to $600 for a card design.

I've had deals in the action-sports market with small companies where I charged a flat fee of $1,500 per image, with a discount if they license more than one image at a time. I've had deals in the tech industry where I charged a $15,000 flat fee for a one-time use license.

It's crazy that you can get so little from one company and so much more from another, but that is the way things work. There are different games being played in different pockets of the world. When you figure it out, you can work it to your advantage.

The flat fee amount that you get will depend upon three factors:

1. the strength of your brand and the value it brings to your Licensee
2. the competition in the industry and
3. what the licensee is willing to pay (and what you are willing to ask for)

Some industries have a lot more in their budget than others. We rarely do anything in the surf industry anymore, because it's a dying industry with very little cash. Our most lucrative licensing deals are in the tech industry, the software industry and the automobile industry, as they have large budgets and are able to pay what we ask.

As with all deals, the most important thing is that you get paid what you feel your art is worth, and that you are happy with the end result.

ADVANCES WITH ROYALTIES

An advance is a dollar amount that an artist is paid up front, payable to the artist at the time of signing the contract. It is later deducted from future royalty payments. If the licensee doesn't sell enough of your products and there are no payouts, you get to keep the advance. The advance should always be considered non-refundable.

Here's a simplified example of how an advance/royalty deal would read in the agreement:

"A non-refundable Advance of $2,500.00 USD is due upon signing. The Royalty is Six Percent (6%)."

Or:

"A non-refundable Advance of $650 USD per image is due upon signing. The Royalty is Six Percent (6%)."

What I love about advances is the most obvious: you receive a payment up front. In most licensing deals, you won't see royalties for a year or more because it takes that long to develop a line, sell it and get it shipped to stores. The advance is money *now*, which is when most of us need it.

What I also love about advances is that it is proof of commitment by the licensee. When they are willing to pay you money up front, it shows that they mean business.

The advance is an insurance policy should something go wrong. It hedges against the possibility that there will never be royalties paid in the future, because if a company is willing to pay an advance, then that means they are committed fully to the product sales.

Without commitment by the licensee, sales might not materialize. Sometimes the products never make it to the marketplace or are dropped from the line. And that means no sales, which means no royalties payable to you, the artist.

One reason we almost always require an advance for Drew's work is that it helps me to weed out the serious from the not-so-serious licensees.

If a company is willing to pay us an advance, I'm convinced of their commitment to the success of the product's sales. How much of an advance should you ask for? It depends on the size of the deal and what the Licensee is willing to pay.

One artist I know that regularly licenses his work, who is very well-known, won't even consider doing a deal without an advance of $10,000 or more. For most of our licensing deals, where Drew is providing existing artwork, we require a minimum of a $6,000 advance. You might be wondering how we came to this number. It is a number that I have found that will provide us with the cash flow we need to spend time on it, and, it's a number that most Licensees will agree to.

But, there have been times when we agreed to $4,000, because that is all that the Licensee would pay. We are flexible for deals that we are very excited about.

Insider Note: $4,000 is a magic number. It's a dollar amount that most companies, large or small, can easily say yes to.

There have also been times that we got more than a $6,000 advance. One of our licensees uses a large number of images, and so we charge an advance of $15,000 every two years when we renew our contract with them. We have worked with them for over ten years, and they have no problem paying it because they know that Drew's images help them sell more products.

We ask for a larger advance for deals where Drew has to do more work up front, such as market research, design and creation of an entire new line of artworks. The amount of the advance will be close to our weekly or monthly rate, depending upon how much time we estimate it will take. Without the proper amount of advance, Drew isn't able to put in the time required to do his best work, and there's no point in doing it at all unless it's his best.

Sometimes we will charge the licensee a fee per image as an advance. For example, if the licensee wants a dozen or more images, we charge $650 per image (with a minimum of ten). A per-image fee enables the licensee to add more images as they need to, and gives the artist financial incentive to do the work involved.

On very rare occasions, we will sign a deal where there is no advance payable up front. However, we would only do that if it's something we are extremely excited about and if there is no work up front on our end. We have found that without an advance up front, the licensee has less reason to put all they have into the sales of the products.

It doesn't matter what you charge as an advance, really. If you only charged someone a $500 advance, and they pay it, it shows that they are serious. And it puts money in your pocket now, rather than having to wait a year or two for the license to mature.

When it comes to renewing a contract, know this: if your artwork is the reason a company is selling a high volume of products, you should be paid well for it. You are solving a problem for them, that they otherwise couldn't solve themselves. That solution is highly valuable in the commercial marketplace. Remember this when it's time to renew a license agreement; at that time, you can ask for more money up front and a higher royalty percentage.

GUARANTEES

Some artists will require a Guarantee in their licensing contract. A Guarantee is a minimum set dollar amount that you will be paid, regardless of sales. For example, every quarter you will be paid a minimum of $2,500, if the royalties owed to you fall below that amount.

Sometimes the Guarantee is a dollar amount paid per year rather than per quarter. You can get creative with the Guarantee; just as with everything else, a Guarantee is negotiable.

THINGS THAT GO WRONG

This is worth repeating, because so many artists miss this and they pay dearly in a loss of income. If the deal you are about to enter into is going to require an excessive amount of work on your end, it's crucial to require an adequate advance or a design fee to cover your time. That way, you don't have to wait the twelve months or more that it takes for royalties to generate before you get paid.

Remember, there are no guarantees that a license will generate any royalties at all. Even when the client is excited to work with you and they make a million promises, things go wrong.

What could go wrong, you ask? Below are a few examples:

Company goes out of business: One year we did a deal with one of the largest toy companies in the U.S. Drew spent weeks working on designs for a kid's skateboard line. The line was advertised in magazines throughout the U.S. We were very excited about it. Then, unexpectedly, the company went bankrupt. The line never made it to the marketplace. There were no sales, and so there were no royalty payments. Luckily, we were paid a generous advance so that Drew's time was covered.

New guy comes in: One time we signed on with a kid's clothing company. They had their Drew Brophy line ready to go, after weeks of work on our end. Then a new partner came in and changed everything. The line never made it to retail and no royalties were generated. We had been paid an advance up front, so we were protected from losing a month's worth of work.

Licensee joins the Navy: One of our first licensing deals was for license plates. The Licensee was a nice young guy. We put time into getting him all the artwork he needed. Then, not even a year later, he decided to quit it all and join the Navy! No royalties were earned, and only a small advance had been paid. We lost money on this one.

The flip side to all of this is that for every deal that isn't successful, there's one that is successful. You have to sign on with many companies because some will be duds and some will be good.

There are no set-in-stone pricing structures for licensing or for art deals. You have to be creative and come up with a deal that works for you and for your client.

NON-TRADITIONAL LICENSING

There are non-traditional ways to license your artwork; many of which do not include the sale of products with your art on them.

One example of a non-traditional deal would be licensing your art for an advertising campaign. The pricing would be determined by the size of the company, the extent of the campaign, and where it will be shown.

If you are licensing your art to a billion dollar tech company for a television campaign, you could get between a $20,000 - $100,000 license fee. If you are licensing to a small company that's valued under a million dollars, for their Facebook advertising, you might be able to get $1,500.

If you are licensing for a beverage company to use your art on their in-store point of purchase displays, you could get in the tens of thousands for one campaign. The range is wide, and each deal has to be considered individually.

When considering what to charge for a non-traditional licensing deal, find answers to these questions: How large is the company (what are they worth $$$), how perfect is my artwork for their campaign, how long will they use it for, where will it be shown.

If you aren't sure what to charge, invest in a consultant who is an expert on pricing. Doing the extra research could make you thousands of dollars more.

19

RUN YOUR ART BUSINESS LIKE A BUSINESS

*"Making money is art and working is
art and good business is the best art."*

—Andy Warhol

One of my favorite quotes is by mega-successful singer Dolly Parton, who said during an interview with Dan Rather, that she tends to "...lay a little heavy on the business side of things." Dolly credits her success to good business decisions.

She explained that early in her music career, she did the unthinkable and turned down a tempting offer from Elvis. Elvis wanted to buy the copyrights to her song "I will always love you." Any other artist would have sold it to the King of Rock and Roll. But not Dolly. She knew that if she owned the rights, she could continue making money off of her song for the rest of her life.

It was a sound decision, because that song became one of the best selling singles of all time. Dolly's heirs will be collecting royalties from it long after she's gone.

In Dolly's interview with Dan Rather she went on to explain that once she saw that she could make money with her music, she realized that she could make music profitable, as long as she made smart business decisions.

She said, "I thought, well, they do call this the music business. So, why don't I kinda lay a little heavy on the business side of things?"

Successful artists generate success by making good decisions. Picasso, Salvador Dali, Andy Warhol; they all placed a focus on making good business decisions, and it did not take away from the validity of their art. The decisions you make on a daily basis are either going to make or break your career.

PROFIT AND CASH FLOW

A former accountant once told me "If you're not making a profit, then what you've got is a hobby."

I'll never forget those words, as they inspired me to set up our art business to always earn a profit. I write about money often, and some people don't like it; they say that artists shouldn't allow their creative minds to become muddled with something as meaningless as money.

Money is a necessary evil; without it, I wouldn't be able to live in my house or feed my kids or pay for art supplies. Our global money system is firmly in place in society and that isn't going to change anytime soon, so we have to either accept it or go live in a cave.

For a full time professional artist, making sales and being paid properly will keep you in business. For the hobby artist, being paid for your work enables you to continue to produce work, as art supplies can be costly.

If you don't care to earn money from your work, then you can skip reading this book entirely, because none of it will apply to you. But, if you are an artist who wants to earn a living with your art, you should know this:

To earn a full time living from your art, you must commit to the mindset of running your art business *like a business*. I have worked with hundreds of artists over the years and I get insight into what they are earning. Many of the artists I work with are earning over $100,000 a year. It is not uncommon for artists to earn six figures selling their art.

I also work with artists earning less than $10,000 a year with their art but are striving to increase that income. There are many differences between the artist earning six figures and those earning less than $10,000, none of which have anything to do with talent.

If you want to earn over six figures a year, read this entire chapter, three times. And then re-read it every month until you reach your income goal.

There are gems of wisdom here that you have to truly "get" before you'll be ready to apply. You will "get it" over time by consistently programming your mind to these concepts.

An art business must have the following three components to be successful:

1. Cash Flow (money coming in)
2. Profit (your money from sales minus your expenses and overhead = profit)

Without Profit, your business will die. Or, in other words, if you aren't making a profit, then what you have is a hobby. This is not a bad thing, but be aware of the difference. *It doesn't matter how much money you bring in, it's how much you keep.*

3. Vision for the future (know what you want, set goals and write it down on paper)

When you make the decision to treat your art business like a business, your mental thoughts and subsequent actions will evolve to stay in line with that decision.

For every project, commission or job that you accept, you will create the intention of generating cash flow and a profit. And when you think that way consistently, every day, you *will* create cash flow and profit.

DETERMINE YOUR INCOME REQUIREMENT

Let me ask you a question: What is your weekly income requirement? What I mean is, what is the minimum amount you need to bring in every week to keep your art business thriving?

If you don't know the answer to that question off of the top of your head, you should. But don't worry, the exercise in this chapter will help you with the answer. There are many methods to determine your income requirements. Below are the two most common:

1. DETERMINE YOUR DESIRED $ AMOUNT AND GO FOR IT METHOD

Decide the yearly and monthly amount you want to earn and then work backwards from that. This method works for some, but you have to have a healthy money relationship and a strong business mind to use it.

For example, an artist who has decided he will earn $200,000 a year with his fine photography will focus all of his efforts on getting at least ten $20,000 projects a year, and say no to everything else. This method can work for someone with the proper mindset, patience and an aggressive manner.

Most people, however, respond better to the second method shown below.

2. BAM + 20% METHOD

BAM stands for "Bare Ass Minimum", a term I borrowed from my wise business coach, Ralph. Determine what you need to earn yearly and monthly to cover your expenses and lifestyle, and then add 20% padding to that number. This method works best for most artists, because it is simple and practical.

HOW TO DETERMINE YOUR SALES GOALS BASED ON BAM + 20% METHOD

(Please note in the example below I'm rounding up so the math is not exact to the penny.)

1. Determine your BAM number

Your BAM number is the amount that you must earn to cover your living and business expenses. Add up your living expenses and your business expenses to determine your yearly BAM number.

For Example: Your yearly BAM is $60,000 to pay living expenses, studio rent, taxes, health insurance, debt repayment, IRA contribution and vacation.

2. Add 20% to your BAM number to generate a minimal amount of profit. The goal is to earn more than 20%, but 20% is good to begin with.

For Example: Your BAM of $60,000 x 20% profit = $12,000. $60,000 BAM + $12,000 Profit = $72,000 total.

That means that $72,000 in sales is your Minimum Yearly Sales Goal.

3. Take your Minimum Yearly Sales goal and break it down into monthly, weekly and daily income requirements:

Example: $72,000 yearly is $6,000 monthly / $1,500 weekly / $300 daily (based on 5 days/week)

Once you know what your weekly and daily "rate" is, you can more easily come up with pricing that is in line with what you need to earn.

Knowing your weekly and daily rate is incredibly helpful when you are asked to do a project that you haven't done before. This is especially useful for artists who do projects that cannot be easily defined in terms of time, but rather in days.

You should review your business each quarter and determine if you have hit your income goals or are far away. If you are not hitting your income goals, then you know that you have more work to do to either sell your work, get new clients or start selling products based on your work.

HOW TO USE THE BAM + 20% METHOD FOR PRICING

There are many different ways to price your work. If the industry or market you work in has a standard, you could choose to follow that standard. Or, you can use this method instead. Below are a few examples.

UNIQUE PROJECTS: For artists who take on unique projects, such as digital illustrations, painting random items or special projects that are difficult to categorize, this example illustrates how to use the BAM + 20% method:

Using the $72,000 per year example above, if someone commissions you for a special project and you estimate that it will take you five days from start to finish, you will charge at a minimum your weekly rate of $1,500 + the cost of supplies and travel and other expenses.

ORIGINAL PAINTINGS: For artists who sell original artworks, this example illustrates how to use the BAM + 20% method: Determine how many days one painting takes you to create, multiply that number by your daily rate, add your art materials expenses to that number, and now you have your retail price for your painting. Determine how that breaks down into square inches (or square centimeters) and use that per square inch, linear inch or per square centimeter price as a base for all of your paintings.

On the next page is a worksheet that will guide you to determining your income goals based on the BAM + 20% method.

INCOME GOALS WORKSHEET

Name: _____ Date_____

Use this worksheet to ensure that every project earns at least your minimum goal for the month, week or day. Every six months, re-visit this worksheet. Raise your prices by 10-20% or more every 12 months.

The Bare Minimum I need to earn yearly to cover daily living expenses plus business expenses including insurance, studio rent, retirement savings and taxes:

Yearly Bare Minimum (BAM) $_____

Determine Yearly Income Goal:

$_____ x 20% = _____

Yearly Bare Minimum (BAM)   Profit Goal

Now Add _____ + _____ = _____

            Yearly BAM   Profit Goal   Yearly Income Goal

Determine Monthly Income Goal: (this is your monthly rate)

$_____ divided by 12 Months = $_____

Yearly Income Goal   Monthly Income Goal

Determine Weekly Income Goal: (this is your weekly rate)

$_____ divided by 4 Weeks = $_____

Monthly Income Goal   Weekly Income Goal

Determine Daily Income Goal: (this is your day rate)

$_____ divided by 5 days = $_____

Weekly Income Goal   Daily Income Goal

20

GETTING PAID

"Money is better than poverty,
if only for financial reasons."

—Woody Allen

If I had to choose the most harmful myth in the art business, I would say it is the prevalent misunderstanding that artists should give their art away in exchange for exposure.

Other people's expectation for cheap art literally robs an artist from their ability to earn a living. Sometimes the thieves are those we love; friends, family and charities.

Many people don't realize that when you give art away consistently, you degrade your art business and devalue your work.

You don't have to give your art away in exchange for recognition. No other business in the world operates this way, and for good reason; it is not sustainable as a business practice.

If you're not careful, you can fall into this trap and get into a consistent habit of giving your work away for less than it's worth. Over time, you will drain your resources to nearly nothing and have to shut down your art business.

There are exceptions to every rule, so yes, there may be a rare time when it makes sense to lower your price or give art to someone special, but, as a daily business practice, "cheap and free = out of business".

The world is full of people who erroneously believe that creating art is not "real" work and that the artist will benefit from giving it away. It's not their fault. They have been conditioned by other artists to think this way. The artists who don't value their own work are setting a precedent for the entire industry.

If you are one of the artists doing this, I don't want to make you feel bad. I want to help you change your ways. You, too, have been a victim of past conditioning. My goal is to give you a new perspective on the exchange of money and forever change the way you work with clients, charities and friends.

Below are the top four art business thieves:

1. The Great Promotion Myth
2. People we love; friends and family
3. Charities
4. Clients with Small Budgets

In the following sections I share strategies that will enable you to prevent these thieves from robbing your dream of being a thriving artist.

The moment you implement the strategies in this section is the moment you will increase your income and you feel empowered and in control of your art business.

Just as the world is full of people who want free art, the world also has a plethora of people who are happy to pay you for your hard work and talent. Your job is to say "no" to the former and seek out the latter.

THE GREAT PROMOTION MYTH

"An artist can die from exposure."
—Author unknown

When someone says "this will be great promotion for you," I cringe. In the world of art, the word "promotion" is code word for "free." It's usually followed with "We don't have a budget for your work, but if you do it for free, you will be exposed to many people."

Moments before I sat down to write this chapter, I received a text from an artist friend in Florida who asked "Is it okay to give my art to a company in exchange for promotion?" My text back to him read, "No. Find out what they want and give them a price quote."

He called me right away. He explained that someone at a local business said that if he painted a wall mural in their corporate headquarters at no charge, they would promote his art. When I pressed him to explain what exactly they will do to promote his art, he said that his name would be on the wall. This is not promotion! Your name always goes on the wall, even if you're paid a million bucks. And so what? Your name is on the wall and about fifty employees get to see it. Not one of them will call you for work, because they aren't your right buyers and because they know you did it for free. So if they do call, they expect you to do it for them for free, too.

There is no such thing as "free in exchange for promotion."

True promotion is when your work is exposed to the masses, either through print, TV, website advertising or some other means to reach large numbers of people, and your name and contact information is clearly visible so the masses can easily find you and buy your work.

When one promises to promote your work, it usually does not mean they will direct people to your website. It rarely means they will make a page on their website dedicated to you and your art. And it never means that they will take out full page ads in a magazine for you.

No company will adequately promote your work for you, no matter what they promise. Not unless you are paying them, or it is written in a contract and they are obligated to do so.

I've seen artists create illustrations for concert posters for free, and then the company didn't even print the artist's name on the poster. There is zero promotion in that. Without a name on the poster, no one knows who did the art.

You should always be paid, even if the work you do provides exposure. When we license Drew's artwork, we get paid, and at the same time, Drew's art and signature is promoted on the products that the art is printed on.

This subject brings out the feisty in me because so many artists fall victim to it. You don't see new doctors giving away free visits to get business. Nor do plumbers give away their services in exchange for promotion. The only world in which we see this is with art.

Why do we see this in art? Because artists keep giving art away, which sets the expectation for all artists. The reason I am so pained by this practice is because I work closely with artists who are struggling. When you give your art away it prevents you from earning a living. It takes away from your family. It literally robs you of your ability to maintain a healthy, thriving business. And if you allow it to continue for too long, it will kill your creative spirit.

When a professional artist gives too freely, they eventually go out of business. We need to change this paradigm. I'm changing it in my world and I encourage you to help me change it for all artists.

HOW TO TURN A REQUEST FOR FREE INTO PAID

I'm surrounded by artists in my line of work. I get to meet the fresh new ones that come out of art school, the mid-career artist and artists who have had lifelong success. But the one artist I worry most about, and the one that I usually can't help, is the senior artist who is bitter and angry, after a lifetime of being taken advantage of.

One artist I worked with, I'll call him "Bob," was mid-sixties. He was extremely talented and had achieved masterful works throughout his life. Bob refused to learn about business and he was continually taken advantage of. After decades of this, Bob had enough. He became bitter and angry and impossible to communicate with.

This is a true story, and I have seen it happen with others. I don't want this to happen to you. From today forward, creatively find ways to get paid for doing promotional or charity work.

Is there ever a time that you should give art away? Maybe. Here is a short list of when I think it's okay to give art for free: to your mother or father, who gave you life; to the donor who gave you a kidney; and to your very best friend that you grew up with and has done big things for you over the years.

There will never be a shortage of opportunities for artists to do free stuff. You can often turn them into a paid gig. When presented by an opportunity, get into the habit of asking yourself: "how much is this going to cost and who is going to pay for it?"

When we ask questions, we find answers.

If an opportunity does not pay you enough to generate cash flow and profit, *turn it down*. Say "no" to people, projects and things that will pull you away from profit-earning projects.

One thing to keep in mind with false opportunities; the person asking for your work for free, has a budget for everything else. They have a budget for printing, rent, advertising, office supplies and business travel. They also have a budget for art, they just don't want to pay you if they don't have to.

A few years ago I received a call from a promoter who was putting on a very high profile event in the Florida Keys. He said that they were investing over a half a million dollars into this event. He boasted that A-Listers like the football celebrity Mike Ditka and comedian Dana Carvey would be present and promised that we would get so much exposure that we would never have to work again. This promise was a red flag to me. How could he possibly know that?

He asked for Drew to create an illustration that would be used for their advertising campaign and merchandise. It would be a four week project for Drew. But here's the kicker; he didn't want to pay for it. I said, "You're investing $500,000 into this event, yet you don't have a budget for art?"

I used to just say "no" when given these "offers" to do work for free. It would make me so angry! But, I've gotten a little wiser with age and now, I turn it into a sale. More than half of the time, I am able to get someone who wanted a donation to pay for it. How? By explaining that what they are asking for will take time, and if they want it to look great, they have to pay.

And if they don't care if the work is professional, they should go to a high school student that's an aspiring artist and help them get practice. Below are scripts on how to turn these requests for a freebie into a sale.

SCRIPTS:

When you get an offer from a potential client to give art in exchange for promotion, follow these steps:

1. Pretend you didn't hear them ask for it for free or cheap. Allow your mind to automatically reject that part of the conversation. This is very important. Pretend you didn't hear it.

2. Listen and ask questions so that you can understand exactly what they need. Once you have all the details, say:

"This is a great opportunity, thank you. I'll write up a proposal and email it to you." This announces that you are viewing them as a client and will provide a price quote.

If they say, "We don't have a budget; we were hoping you would donate it," then say: "Based on what you just told me, you'll need a professional artist to do this for you. Let me write a proposal for you and if you really need what I have to offer, then you'll find a way to budget for it. Fair enough?"

Sometimes, the client suddenly comes up with money for it, because they really need it and they want you to be the one to do it. Other times, they say "sorry, we don't have any money."

And in that case, I either:

1. Recommend they find an artist still in high school to do it, as the young artist may need to add to their portfolio.

2. Brainstorm to find other ways for them to pay for the work. Large companies have many different budgets. If their budget for art is depleted, they will have a budget for advertising and promotion, and you can suggest that they take from that budget.

3. Encourage them to get a sponsor or to do fund-raising to pay for it.

Below is an example of how we handled an opportunity with a company that had no budget for art:

Drew and I used to go to Hawaii every year for a large surfing contest. Ever since he was a teen, it had been Drew's dream to illustrate the art for the contest poster. One year, the promoters called and asked Drew to do the artwork—his dream come true! But there was one problem; they didn't have a budget for art. I asked the promoter, "Do you have a travel budget?" He said, "Yes." I said, "Well, how about this; you pay for our tickets and lodging to Hawaii, in exchange for the illustration. Would that work for you?" And they agreed! It was a win for us, as Drew and I were planning to travel to Hawaii anyway. With this arrangement, we actually got paid more in travel costs than if we were paid in dollars. It was a win-win all around.

FRIENDS AND FAMILY

When a friend or family member asks for your art at no charge, this can feel uncomfortable. It's hard to say "no" to someone we love. But when we say "yes" to giving our work away, we say "no" to our own goals, business and future.

One artist friend of mine is overly generous giving his artwork away, and because of that, he never had the money to help his own daughter pay for college, which he always regretted. Imagine that—unconsciously making choices that take away from your own children.

It's not being greedy when you charge friends and family for your work; it's your profession! When anyone takes work from you and they do not pay for it, they are stealing from your livelihood and your business.

On the other hand, when your friends and family buy from you, they are supporting your work. It's a very loving and generous thing to do.

So, how do we allow ourselves to be generous with others, but yet not go broke over it? The answer is simple; offer a "friends and family discount."

Decide how much of a "friends and family discount" you wish to give to those who are very close to you. It's up to you. We often use a 20% discount. That allows us to be generous, but not to give too much that it hurts our business.

SCRIPT FOR GOOD FRIENDS & FAMILY:

When a good friend wants art from Drew, we feel appreciation for their support of our business.

We tell them: "Thank you so much for your support! Since you're a close friend, I'm happy to offer you a 20% discount off of my regular price."

This response demonstrates that you appreciate that they are supporting your business. It also allows you to be very generous by offering a deep discount.

If it's a $2,000 art piece, a 20% discount is equal to $400. That's incredibly generous to give a friend $400! And, it doesn't break the bank for us.

CHARITY REQUESTS

Recently I received this email from an artist in despair:

"Maria, I get three or four free art requests a week. I'm a cancer survivor and I can't say no, but my business is failing! It is draining me from my being able to support my family and pay my studio rent."

If you have been in business as an artist for more than a year, you most likely are being asked to donate art to every charity, school event and local auction in town.

And chances are, you have a hard time saying no.

Giving to a worthy cause feels great. But, too many artists are giving too much and it creates a financial hardship. This need to give, give, give without thought to what you are losing is part of the "starving artist" paradigm.

If you are giving too much, this section will forever change your perspective and your life. I'm going to give you strategies to handle charity requests that will result in an increase in your income while helping others at the same time.

Artists, photographers, musicians, writers; we make what we do look too easy. That is why our friends, family and even strangers ask us to donate our valuable time and art, not realizing that this is what we do for a living.

When you choose to give mindlessly to others, you take from your own business and family. It doesn't have to be that way. Instead, give mindfully, so that everyone will benefit and you can feel good about it.

HOW TO GIVE MINDFULLY

Drew and I get barraged with charity requests through Facebook and e-mail. Some people even walk into the studio and interrupt Drew while he's working. If you've been a professional artist for more than a few years, this is happening to you regularly.

But wait, isn't giving noble? I have to stop for a moment and share my philosophy on giving to charities and good causes, because if I don't, someone is going to write to me and say "don't be selfish, Maria! Be more giving!"

Yes, giving is noble. Harming your own business to give to everyone else is not. Years ago Drew and I would give art to many charities. In 2008, when the economy crashed, we suddenly had nothing left to give. That's when we took a hard look at where we had been putting our money and time.

Now, instead of giving art to anyone who asks, we choose three charities a year that are near and dear to our hearts, and we pay 10% of our income to them. We mindfully plan out how we will help the causes that we care about.

We all should be generous and help charitable causes, mindfully and in a way that doesn't harm our business or family.

WHY MONEY IS A BETTER DONATION THAN ART

I'm not saying we never give anything other than 10% of our income. Sometimes a local school will ask for a donation for the graduation auction and we will give them posters that we have a large supply of, or something else that's small and inexpensive.

Practically speaking, though, artists fare better by donating money instead of art. This is because artists forget how much their art, time, materials, blood sweat and tears, are worth.

When you give art away consistently, you lose track of how much it's really costing you. Giving money, instead of art, is better because:

1. Donating money is more easily tracked and controlled than art. You can track donations and be in complete control of your finances when writing checks rather than giving away paintings.
2. Donating money is a sensible write-off on taxes. In the USA, the I.R.S. does not value an artist's time creating art, and that lack of value is reflected in tax laws. If you donate $1,500 cash, the IRS gives you a $1,500 write off. However, if you donate a $1,500 painting, the IRS only allows you to write off your actual cost of materials; you cannot write off the value of the three weeks that it took to paint it.

DONATING YOUR ART IN EXCHANGE FOR PROMOTION

Years ago we donated often, freely, for many different charity events. It cost us a lot of time and money, but we were drawn in, wanting to contribute to others. We also thought the promotional aspect that the charities promised could be good for our business.

Over time, we realized that we never got new, paying clients directly from a charitable donation. What we did get, though, were more and more requests to donate art.

The idea that giving art away is going to get you more business is false. If you are donating for promotional purposes, you're doing it for the wrong reasons.

TURN IT INTO A SALE

So what do you do with all of these requests for art for charity? Turn it into a sale.

Charitable organizations are run like any other business; they have a product (their promise), a vision and a brand. They need a logo and design, a lawyer and a website. And if they want these things done right, they have to pay for them. If they want artists to donate their best work for auction, they will have to financially reimburse the artist. Otherwise, artists will give their worst pieces, and this doesn't do anyone any good.

Below are strategies to turn a charity request into a sale:

1. AUCTION ITEMS: When a charity asks for a donation for their auction, give them these options to choose from:

A. Sell the item to them at a wholesale price, and anything they earn over that price is their donation. Payment is due at pick up or delivery, or, due three (3) business days after the auction.

B. Agree to a 50/50 split of the auction proceeds. Make sure you set the starting bid price. If the item doesn't sell, you require it back in your possession within three business days. If the item sells, your 50% cut is due within three business days. Their 50% is your donation.

   Some charities will tell you that their by-laws don't allow for a split of auction; in this case, then a wholesale price will have to do. The discount off the retail price is your donation to the charity.

C. Offer a gift certificate as a donation for $100 off the buyer's purchase of a $500 or higher priced artwork from you. With this option, you are only donating $100, but you truly do get new business when the buyer comes to purchase a piece of art from you. Some artists will include a small, inexpensive art print to go with the certificate, so that a representation of their art will be on display for the auction.

Last year, a local private school asked Drew for a donation of artwork for their annual auction. We had an original painting which we offered to the school at a wholesale price of $1,200. The retail value was $2,500. We agreed to take the art back if they didn't sell.

A few days after the auction, my contact at the school brought me a $1,200 check. She said that the piece sold for $5,000! The school made $3,800 off of that donated art piece. I would say that was a generous donation.

2. DESIGN, website or illustration work: Take the time to find out what they need; get a good understanding of their problem and then put together a proper proposal.

Tell them that you are happy to offer a 10% or 20% discount off your normal rate; this is your donation. For example, a $1,000 project discounted at 20% = a $200 donation. This is a very generous donation for an artist to make.

Don't feel bad about charging charities for your work. Everyone else is getting paid, and they don't feel bad about it. The employees at the charities don't feel bad cashing their paychecks, nor do their attorneys feel remorse for charging legal fees, nor does their printer, their landlord, or any other vendor.

If the charity does not accept your proposal or your offer, that's okay, let them go. Out of the many charities that contact us, only about 50% actually buy from us. The rest of them find artists who are willing to give art away.

DESIGN FOR A CHARITY

A few years ago a dear friend of mine asked Drew to create an illustration package for his charity. They needed logo treatments, a full illustration and t-shirt designs. It was going to take Drew at least four weeks from start to finish.

I was excited and said, "Thank you so much for the opportunity! I'll work up a proposal for you."

He said, "Oh, we were hoping Drew would do it for free." My enthusiasm dropped like a lead balloon! I explained to my friend, "What you are asking for is an entire month's income from us. He countered, "But thousands of people will see the art. It will be great promotion for you!"

I jokingly suggested, "Why don't you just donate a month of your income to the charity, and that can pay for the art?" He went silent. This helped to put it into perspective for him. And then he said, apologetically, "Wow, I never looked at it like that."

I told him I would provide him with a proposal with a discount. I assured him that there would be no hard feelings if the charity decided not to accept our proposal and use someone else.

A week later, my friend called to say that the charity accepted our proposal. They decided not to use a cheaper, inexperienced illustrator, because this project was going to be highly publicized and it had to look great. Drew completed the project, and it was a win-win for everyone.

I didn't lose a friend for saying "no freebies" and I didn't put my business and my family in jeopardy by giving away a month's income. Instead, we gave a "donation" via a 20% discount to a good charity, the client was happy AND we got paid. It worked out great for all involved.

SCRIPTS FOR CHARITIES

W you get a request to donate your art, instead of thinking "oh no, not again," see it as an opportunity to put these strategies into practice.

When you respond to someone with confidence, such as "Here's what I offer to charities..." their response will be one of respect and understanding.

Script #1 – Turn their Request for Auction Artwork into a Sale:

"Thank you for your interest in my art. I am happy to provide one of my best pieces for your event. This is how I work with charities; I'm able to donate 50% of the retail price of the art piece you choose. The other 50% will be payable to me at pickup or delivery. Any money your charity earns over the 50% that you pay is all yours. Fair enough?"

GIFT CERTIFICATES are your next best option: If the charity says, "No thank you, we don't have a budget to purchase art," your next option is to offer a Gift Certificate, not an actual art piece.

This way, the charity earns their money off the auction, and you gain a new art buyer and a sale when the buyer comes to cash in their certificate.

Script #2 – Turn their Request for Free Design/Illustration Work into a Sale:

Script: "Thank you for your interest in working with me. I appreciate the opportunity. Can you tell me a little more about what you need?" (This is asked so you can assess what they need and then you can put together a detailed proposal that shows how you can solve their design problems.)

Ask questions so that you gain an understanding of what their problem or challenge is and what their desired result is. Then say: "Thanks for the detail. I am confident I can create art to meet your needs." (Explain how you can get them the results they need.)

Then continue, "Your charity is doing important work, and so I'd like to make a donation that's equal to 20% of the cost of the work. I'll write up a proposal and send it to you and we can go from there. Sound good?"

The above script establishes two things:

1. that you recognize how important their charity is, and that you are willing to donate in the form of a discount, and;
2. that you expect them to pay you for your services.

Setting up the expectation changes the dynamic of future communications. Your proposal should then show the total cost, and then indicate the discount (donation) that you offer, and a total after that amount is deducted.

THE SMALL BUDGET

When a client says "I have a small budget", what you think you hear them saying is that they want you to give them a cheaper price than you do everyone else.

This is the first mistake; assuming that you know what the client means. Without knowing how much money they are willing to spend, you can't possibly know what their actual budget is.

Many of us make the mistake of thinking someone else's budget is the same as ours. What I think is too expensive for me, would be considered affordable to someone in a higher income bracket. You can't put your own budget restrictions onto your client.

I've had many instances where a client's "small budget" turned out to be more money than what we quoted them. A small or large budget is different for each person.

One summer I had a collector call and ask how much it would cost for a commission. She started the conversation by saying "I can't afford a lot, but I thought I'd ask how much Drew would charge for a 36"x48" painting." At the time, we charged $3,600 for a commission that size. When I told her the price, I expected her to say she couldn't afford it. But instead, she said, "Oh, that's cheaper than I thought. Great, let's get started."

On the other hand, some clients truly can't afford your prices. When a client asks for a price quote and mentions they are on a tight budget, just give a price quote for the work they requested. Their budget is irrelevant to your prices, because your prices are what they are.

If, after giving the quote, they say they have a budget smaller than your price, don't make the mistake of giving them what you quoted for a lower price. If you do, you are lowering the value of your work and you will financially harm your business. You will also send a message to the client that your pricing is bogus.

If they suggest you charge a cheaper price now and they will pay full price later, do not fall for that one. Once you set a price precedent, the client always expects the same prices later. Instead of lowering your price, convince your client of the value so they increase their budget and pay full price. Often, a client's budget is reflective of how much trust they have in you.

If they truly want your work, but they aren't completely confident that you can do it the way they want, you have to take the time to convince them. Many times I've been able to get a client to increase their budget after gaining their trust that we are capable of producing what they need.

The way you convince them that you are capable is by talking to them. Have a lengthy conversation, ask a lot of questions, and then parrot back to them what they said they need. This shows that you listened and understand. If they feel that you understand them, they will have more confidence in you. Then, tell them about a previous client whom you worked with on a similar project and how it was a huge success.

Explain that you want to give them the best quality work possible, but the only way you can do it is if they increase their budget to allow you the time required. A lower price cuts back on your time and materials and will not allow you to do your best for them.

If they still cannot increase their budget, then tell them that the next best option is to lessen the scope of work so that it matches their budget. Often Drew will have someone ask him to paint their surfboard. They will want a full board painting and a lot of detail. Then he will price it out as a full painting, and they say they can't afford it.

Rather than letting the customer go, Drew will ask, "What is your budget? I'll give you a painting to match it." If their budget is a fraction of the cost of the full board painting, he will paint a very small painting on the nose of their surfboard instead.

It's not exactly what they wanted, but, it gives them what they can afford. Always brainstorm to find a way to get your client close to what they want, working within their budget, without you eating the loss.

You can meet their budget by lessening the scope of work, going smaller, using less expensive materials, use less detail, etc. Take the time to figure out how to cut back on time and materials to work with their budget.

Another way to help a client with a tight budget is to offer payment options. Have them pay 30% up front and then make monthly payments thereafter. Have them sign a payment agreement and give you a credit card number. You can automatically charge their card each month when their payment is due.

If the options above don't appeal to your client, then refer them to an artist who is still in school and looking to build their portfolio. This doesn't do anything for you personally, but you will be helping out a new artist and at the same time solving the problem of a would-be client.

Be sure to maintain a friendly and professional attitude with every client, even those who can't afford your services. Wish them well, and let them know you'll be happy to work with them if their financial situation changes. Be genuine and kind. If their experience with you was pleasant, they may come back to you later with a larger budget.

Clients who go to artists who charge cheap prices often do not get what they need and will end up coming back to you, once they realize they need a professional. At that time, their budget suddenly grows. Welcome them back and handle it gracefully. We've had this happen many times.

Once a company wanted Drew to create a poster for their surfing contest. It was a rush-job and they needed the art in two weeks. We gave them a price quote and they said they couldn't afford it, so they hired another artist. Two weeks later, they called Drew in a panic. They said the artist they hired didn't do a good job and now they were desperate and needed the art in two days. We gave them a new price quote and added a rush fee, because getting it done that quickly would mean no sleep for Drew for 48 hours. Now, they suddenly had to increase their budget plus had to pay an extra 20% rush fee.

21

TRAIN PEOPLE HOW TO TREAT YOU

"We tend to get what we expect."
—Norman Vincent Peal

About 10 years ago, a local surfboard shaper and Drew made a trade. One painting for one surfboard. Some time later, the surfboard shaper drove by another local business and saw that the art on his Brophy painting had been printed on a poster and it hung in their window.

He immediately drove to our studio and stormed into the front door, yelling "That's my art! That's my art! How dare you sell my art to someone else!"

Drew looked at him and said, "How do you think I feed my family?" And then went on to explain to the shaper that if he limited his sale of surfboard shapes to just one guy, he wouldn't be able to make a living. To stay in business, he has to sell his surfboard shapes to many people, not just one. The art business works the same way.

The man stopped and realized the absurdity of his anger. He calmed down, and came to understand. Most of our clients know that we have a business model of reproducing and licensing art. They have come to expect that if the piece of art they bought has mass appeal, they will see art prints of it become available. We have trained the public to be accustomed to our business model.

Those that aren't okay with our business model may not understand this business, and so we have to take time to help them understand. And yes, some people will disagree with our business model, and that is okay.

Not everyone understands art, and even less understand the business of it.

But don't let someone's misunderstanding of the art business change your business model. Instead, stand firm in your decisions and overall plan and be the example to others as to how it's done.

HOW TO TRAIN PEOPLE

Drew always says, "you train people how to treat you." People come to expect what you expect, and they will fulfill that expectation. This can work in your favor, or not, depending on how you choose to make your expectations known.

I've seen this truth unfold many times. One example is the relationship we have with the company Liquid Force. Drew designed wakeboards for them years ago. After a few years of not working with them, they called asking to commission Drew once again for new designs. We agreed on pricing, and our contact, Jimmy, said, "I know Drew won't start until he gets a deposit, so I'll have accounting cut a check right away." He's worked with Drew in the past, and he remembers that Drew expects partial payment before he begins the work.

You can train people to treat you the way you want to be treated by:

1. Being verbally clear of your expectations in the very beginning.
2. Being consistent in your policies (pricing policies, meeting deadlines, expecting payment on time).
3. Valuing your own time enough to not allow people to waste it.
4. Setting boundaries and sticking to them, without apology.

Word gets around and over time, all of the people in your life will get used to your expectations and treat you accordingly. They come to expect your expectations, and they fulfill it.

THE BAD CLIENT

One artist I worked with wanted help dealing with a bad client. She said the client paid her well, but they had a dysfunctional relationship. Her client would text her at all hours of the day and night and even on weekends. She felt compelled to answer their texts within minutes, or they would hound her. She felt like she was trapped, with no free time for herself or her family. She said it was like having a bad boyfriend.

The root of the problem was the artist, not the client. She had trained her client to treat her this way, by not setting boundaries in the very beginning. She had answered every single text within minutes, even on her off-work time. By doing so, she gave them a signal that she had no personal life and that it was okay to do this.

I suggested that she re-train them by setting specific work hours for herself and sticking to it. I advised her to send her bad boyfriend client an email saying:

"I wanted to inform you that for greater efficiency, I have restructured my work schedule. Starting immediately, I will be available Monday through Friday, between the hours of 9 a.m. and 5 p.m. If you need to send a communication to me during a non-work time, please know that I will respond as soon as possible on the following work day."

Just like puppies and kids, it's easier to train a client in the beginning. When you form a relationship with a new client, clearly tell them what your expectations and boundaries are. Most people will respect your expectations and give you what you ask for.

22

HOW TO PRICE YOUR ARTWORK

It would be so easy if there was a book out there that told you what to charge, wouldn't it? Well, there is one for the commercial artist and it's by The Graphic Artist's Guild titled *Handbook: Pricing and Ethical Guidelines.* This book should be owned by every artist, as it contains general pricing guidelines and a plethora of written agreements that you can use. One caveat: some of the pricing guidelines seem to be too low, and others sometimes seem too high. But in their defense, pricing is based on so many different factors that it's impossible to write a book that applies to everyone. I recommend using the book as a guide, but come up with pricing that is most appropriate for your work.

The price of your artwork will be based on many different factors, including:

1. The market you choose to sell your work in (high end versus low end)
2. The medium you use
3. Your level of mastery
4. The strength of your name or brand and the demand for your work
5. The time involved
6. The industry standards for the type of work you do

Pricing varies from artist to artist for all of the factors listed above. I have friends who sell their original paintings for as low as $200 each, and I have friends who sell their paintings for $10,000. Sometimes the difference between the $200 painting and the $10,000 painting is hard to see. In art, pricing doesn't always make logical sense.

Since the artists reading this book range from photographers to illustrators to fine artists, I can't possibly cover all pricing in this book. Instead, I'll share a few pricing guidelines that will be helpful for most of you.

PRICE IN THE HIGH END
VS.
LOW END MARKETS

When determining your pricing, you might be surprised to know that you can actually decide which market you will sell your work in. You can make the choice to either sell higher priced works or to sell lower priced works.

Your decision on which market you'll sell your work goes back to what you want, as we discussed in the first chapter in this book.

If you want your artwork to appeal to celebrities and be sold for $20,000 or more, then that is where your focus should be. To sell in the high end market, you'll have to use the finest of materials and develop mastery at your craft. You'll have to form business relationships with people in that market. You'll have to avoid venues where low price work is being sold.

If you want your work to bring joy to as many people as possible and you want anyone to be able to afford it, then that is where your focus should be. To sell to the mass markets, your work would have to be priced on the mid to lower end so more people can afford it.

I was at a local street fair recently and I visited the booth of a talented artist selling beautiful, hand crafted wood furniture. I remembered him from last year at the same fair; Drew and I bought two of his hand crafted stools for our studio. One thing that I noticed about his work is that it would sell very well in the high end market. But, here he was selling it at a street fair, priced too low. His small wooden chairs were priced at $200 each. I know that the amount of time this this gifted artist put into making each chair was worth well beyond what he was charging. He could be selling through designers in Laguna Beach, a nearby town where people with large homes and high incomes would love his work.

Maybe he doesn't know that he can choose to hit the high end market instead. If I were coaching him, I would recommend that he no longer sell at street fairs and triple his prices. He could call on interior designers and art consultants in wealthy areas in the county. He could form a relationship with those professionals and sell his work at premium prices to homeowners that would love the work, and have the money to afford it.

Raising his prices would allow him to include a commission for the interior designers and consultants so that they have incentive to connect him with their premium clients. It would also pay him more adequately for his fine work. When prices are higher, it makes your art more interesting to wealthier people. If it's priced too low, you give the impression that it is worth less than it truly is.

Everything you do with your business is a choice, including to whom you choose to sell to.

When you decide to sell your work at a flea market, you are making a choice of who you want your customers to be. As such, you have to charge prices at a lower amount to make it sell to the customers in that market.

When you decide to sell to the high end market, you will have to sell your work in places where that high end customer shops. As such, your prices will have to be high enough to attract the high end customer.

Please know, there is nothing right or wrong with either choice. I know many artists who make a great living selling in the lower priced market. Some artists' work is entirely appropriate to sell at street fairs, and some would not be.

For example, jewelry designers. Some use low priced materials, imitation stones and China-sourced charms for their jewelry; this would sell best at a local craft fair and would be priced on the low end. An artist who creates jewelry using gemstones, fine metals and a unique style would price her pieces on the high end through galleries, fine art shows and boutique stores.

You have to decide for yourself where you want to put your focus. Your decision should be based on what you want for the future of your art business.

HOW TO COME UP WITH PRICING

Some artists have no idea what their prices are. They have different prices for different clients and projects. The problem with not having a consistent price structure is that you'll often underprice your work. It also makes it difficult to discuss price with potential clients. And, lastly, it will be confusing to everyone.

Take the time to come up with a consistent pricing structure, one that you can memorize and explain to your clients. You can change your prices anytime. If you find that your pricing is too low, adjust it.

Pricing is best when based on something that can be measured, such as by the square foot or square inch, by materials used or by time blocks.

If you are not sure of where to begin with pricing, base your prices on the current market value. Research what the public is paying for the work of artists similar to yours. Use their pricing as a baseline and make adjustments to the pricing to be in line with your own mastery level.

Your price structure should remain the same regardless of where you are selling the art. If you are selling art in galleries, those prices should be formulated the same as the prices you are offering when selling directly to collectors. You cannot have two different price structures, as it will create a problem for the gallery and confuse the public.

Keep in mind, what one artist believes is a high price for a piece of art, another thinks is too low. Money and pricing is all relative to where you are with your mindset, your market and your background.

Many artists are afraid to talk about how much they charge. They fear competition or judgment. I don't believe in competition when it comes to art. Art is so unique and personal that there is no way to compete. There is never going to be another Drew Brophy, even if someone tries. And there is never going to be another you.

PRICING PAINTINGS

Below are two different ways to price paintings. I used the example of $6.00 per square inch for oil paintings because I know many oil painters that charge about that plus framing. However, the numbers shown are just examples. You will have to come up with your own pricing that works best for you.

Oil paintings are priced higher than acrylics and watercolors. Watercolors are priced higher than acrylics but lower than oils. If you are painting in various mediums, you would create different price structures for each. Also, if you are painting on paper, it tends to sell for less than a painting on canvas.

Pricing paintings by the Square Inch:

To price by the square inch, multiply the length of the painting by the height to get the total square inches. Then, multiply your square inches by your per-square-inch price.

Example: Painting is sized 8"x10". Eight inches multiplied by ten inches equals 80 square inches. Multiply 80 by your per square inch price of $6.00 and your total painting price is $480.00. Round your price up to the nearest dollar, $500.

Using the per square inch method, your painting prices may look like this:

- 6"x8"=60 square inches x $6.00 = $360, round down to $350
- 11"x14"=154 square inches x $6.00 = $924, round down to $900
- 18"x24"=432 square inches x $6.00 = $2,592 round up to $2,600

Sometimes using a per-square-inch price structure doesn't work, particularly if you are an artist who paints on a wide range of sizes. As you can see, the various size examples above, using the per-square-inch pricing, provides for a huge price fluctuation between the smaller paintings and the larger ones.

If you want something with less variation, you can charge by the Linear Inch instead. This pricing structure actually makes a lot of sense, and I just learned about it last year by reading a blog post by Melissa Dinwiddie, on www. TheAbundantArtist.com.

Pricing paintings by the Linear Inch:

To price by the linear inch, you would add the length of the painting by the height to get the total linear inches. Then, multiply your linear inches by your per-linear-inch price. For this example we will use a price of $27.00 per linear inch.

Example: Painting is sized 8"x10". Eight inches plus ten inches equals 18 linear inches. Multiply 18 by your per-linear-inch cost of $27.00 and your total painting price is $486.00. Round your price up to the nearest dollar, which in this example is $500.

Using the per linear inch method, charging $27 per linear inch, your painting prices will look like this:

6"x8"=14 linear inches x $27.00 = $378, round up to $400

11"x14"=25 linear inches x $27.00 = $675, round up to $700

18"x24"=42 linear inches x $27.00 = $1,134 round down to $1,100

ADD FRAMING TO THE PRICE

If you frame the artwork, take the framing cost and multiply it by two. For example, if the frame cost is $60, multiply that by 2 and add $120 to the cost of the painting.

The reason for doubling your frame cost is this: when selling through a gallery or retail store, you will share your sale price 50/50 with the gallery. Even if selling direct to collectors, you want to keep your pricing stable regardless of where you are selling the work.

TIME BLOCK PRICING

For random projects that cannot be structured because they are so unique, we price based on the size of the project. We estimate the amount of time it will take and multiply that by Drew's weekly rate, and often add padding to it, because as you know, everything always takes longer than planned.

A few years ago an eclectic art lover brought Drew a female mannequin to paint. That was difficult to price because we had no idea what was involved with painting a mannequin. We decided to charge our weekly rate times two, as we estimated it would take Drew about 6-8 days to paint.

Refer to your worksheet on setting your income goals to determine your daily and weekly rate. Using time blocks to price out projects is an easy solution to not knowing what to charge. Using the example of an income goal of $72,000 a year, your weekly rate is $1,500 a week. If you are offered a project that you estimate will take two weeks, charge $3,000 plus your expenses. If the project is estimated to take 3 days, charge your daily rate of $300 x 3 = $900 plus expenses. Always pad your timing a little, as things can take longer than planned. If a two week project took one and a half weeks, and you feel guilty for overcharging, you can always refund your client. But if you proposed it would take two weeks and it took three, it's hard to charge your client more after the fact.

RAISING PRICES

The time to raise prices is when your work is in high demand and when the cost of your materials go up. If you are having trouble completing all of the work that is coming to you, that's a sign to raise your prices immediately.

If your prices are the same as they were three years ago, evaluate what you're charging. The price of everything has gone up, including food and housing. Your prices should reflect that.

Don't be afraid to raise your prices with existing clients. Let them know that you are raising your prices to stay in line with inflation and the increased cost of doing business.

23

COMMISSIONED WORKS

"Honest poverty is a gem that even a King
might call his own, but I wish to sell out."
—Mark Twain

A commissioned work is when a client asks you to create something custom just for them, instead of buying what you have already created. Some clients will have a specific idea of what they want the theme, color scheme or size to be.

Most of Drew's paintings are commissioned. Some of our clients aren't very specific about what they want painted. They will give vague instructions, such as, "I like how you paint your suns and your big waves. Just paint me something with those in there." We love when a client gives Drew freedom to create however he wants, as that's when he does his best work.

Other clients will be very specific about what they want. One client, who is an animal biologist, commissioned a beach scene with turtles and his family on the beach in the background. Since Drew's work is surreal in nature, the family was painted as silhouettes on the beach and the turtles in the foreground. We named this painting *Turtle Beach*. This painting appealed to so many people, that we decided to make it available as canvas reproductions. We removed the two children figures in the art from the digital file, showing only the two adults in the piece. It has become a popular image for reproduction sales.

When someone commissions a piece, even if they direct what is being painted, the artist still owns the copyrights to the artwork and retains reproduction rights. With Drew's work, if the painting appeals to the masses, we will make print reproductions of it. Sometimes we will license it for products as well. This is how we leverage Drew's time and earn money off of a painting more than once.

SELLING OUT

Some artists agonize over whether or not they should paint what other people ask them to paint. They worry that by doing so, they are compromising their artistic purpose.

I met a young artist on the beach in South Carolina one summer. She told me that she had quit her job, got a business loan and started her art business. She felt fortunate that she was already selling art and getting a lot of commissions, but one thing worried her. A lot of her clients asked her to paint things she normally wouldn't paint. She asked, "Am I selling out if I paint dogs? I don't like painting dogs."

This idea of *selling out* has always baffled me. Some people think that selling out means you earn money from selling your work commercially. Some think it's when you create what others tell you to. Selling out is none of this.

Selling out is when you agree to do something that goes against your personal values, just for money. For every single person, selling out is different, because we all have very different personal values.

A person who doesn't believe in drinking alcohol would be selling out if they accepted a commission from a liquor company. A person who despises corporate greed is selling out when they accept a large grant that's funded by Microsoft.

Painting subject matter that your client asks you to isn't selling out. Most artists will benefit from the opportunity to experiment in different styles, mediums and subject matter, while being paid to do it.

They may be asked to paint something they normally wouldn't, only to discover a spark of energy, one that wakes up a part of them, and through that exercise they discover something that they love.

Experimenting can open an entire new world of possibilities for an artist. And at the same time, you don't have to go back to that old job that doesn't do anything for your art career, because you are earning money with your art.

WHEN SHOULD YOU NOT ACCEPT A COMMISSION

If it goes against your personal values, don't do it. Or, if a client asks you to create something that you know you are not very good at, then refer it out to another artist.

Sometimes Drew will be requested to paint a portrait. Drew is not a portrait artist, so we will refer those commissions to other artists whom we know will do a great job with it.

After you are fully established and you have a distinctive style, you may decide to no longer accept commissions that require you to stray from your own style.

While Drew is fully capable of painting in other styles, at this point in his career, he chooses not to. When a client asks for something in a different style, we tell them that Drew prefers to paint in his own style. They can then decide if they want to have Drew do it or find another artist.

HOW TO HANDLE THE BUSINESS OF A COMMISSION

When a client asks you to create a commissioned piece of work, follow these steps for a smooth transaction. The steps shown below uses a painting commission as an example. But you can replace the painting details with details that fit your situation, for illustration, digital design, sculpture, etc.

CONVERSATION & UNDERSTANDING: First things first; have a detailed conversation. Ask enough questions so that you get a full understanding of what they want, regarding size, colors, theme, orientation (vertical or horizontal) and any other detail that you need to know.

After you have gained an understanding of what they want, communicate to them how you work. Tell them that you will write up a price quote and send it by email or text. Tell them that once you receive their installment payment, you'll begin work on the sketches.

It's important to let them know in the first conversation that you will begin work after the installment is paid. This way, you avoid misunderstanding. The installment payment is a green light for you to get started.

If you don't have set pricing on what they are asking for, do not give a price quote in the first conversation. This is where most artists under-price themselves, because they haven't taken the time to price it out properly before blurting out a dollar amount that they later regret.

Once you give a price, it's hard to come back later and give a higher amount. If they ask you how much it will be and you aren't 100% sure, tell them "I will have to research my costs and get back to you on that."

If you do have set pricing, for example, you know that for an 18"x24" canvas painting you charge $1,800, then you can tell them the price. But still, you want to follow up in writing so that you can write up all the other details, such as how many sketches are included, the copyright information, how much sales tax will be added and how much shipping will cost. Writing out the details are important, so that there are no misunderstandings later.

PRICE QUOTE: Write up a price quote and send it by email or text. I find email to be easier, but some people prefer text. If you do send it by text, keep a copy of what you sent.

Thank your client for the opportunity and be sure the price quote includes the following (the numbers below can be changed as needed, these are just examples):

A. DESCRIPTION includes their requested details, size, medium and any other detail necessary (i.e. Turtles on the beach with mother, father and two children; large wave and bright sun in background. Father holding fishing rod, painted vertically on 24"x36" gallery wrapped canvas.)

B. PRICE (i.e. Price is $2,500 plus shipping and 8% sales tax. A 50% non-refundable installment payment of $1,250 is payable to begin the sketch process. Add 4% to the total for credit card or Paypal payments. Full balance is due upon completion of work. Artwork will be shipped/delivered/available for pick up upon receipt of balance due.)

Note: I was advised by one attorney to use the word "installment" rather than "deposit" because according to some laws in the U.S., an installment can be considered non-refundable while a deposit sometimes cannot.

It's important for the installment payment to be non-refundable, to protect yourself from a client who changes their mind after you spend hours working on their commission. I had this happen once, and we were stuck with a painting that was very personal to the client and couldn't resell it. We took a little comfort knowing that at least we were paid 50% up front which partially covered the time and materials spent on it.

C. SKETCH PROCESS: (i.e. Sketches will be provided for client's approval or changes. Up to three sketches are included in price. Any sketch changes beyond the third sketch incurs an additional sketch fee of $200 per sketch.)

D. COPYRIGHT NOTICE (i.e. Artist retains all copyrights and reserves the right to reproduce artwork in any manner in the future.)

E. TIMING (i.e. Allow two to three weeks delivery after final sketch approval.)

SKETCH PROCESS: Once your client submits the installment payment, you can begin the sketch or concept process.

One exception to this rule is if you are brand new at the art business and you do not have a portfolio and your client is not sure if you can do the job; in this case, you might you have to convince them to trust you, and you can do that by working up a sketch and showing them. If submitting sketches before the installment gets you the job, then do that. And then, once they approve the sketch, require your 50% installment payment before beginning the rest of the work.

On every sketch, sign your name and copyright notice, like this: "Artwork (c) Drew Brophy".

No one has the right to take your sketches and do what they want with them, not without your approval. Writing your name and (c) notice on the sketch announces that the art in the sketch is owned by you.

For the sketch process itself, every artist has a different way of doing it. The way we handle it is, Drew will work up two to three rough concepts with different layouts and then send those to the client via text or email. Then the client can choose their favorite concept and ask for changes if need be.

After that first feedback, Drew will refine the sketch and submit one follow up sketch for their approval or last bit of changes.

One reason we limit sketches to three is so that the client is motivated to be crystal clear on what they want in the very beginning. In the past, we didn't limit sketches and we would have some clients change their minds over and over again, resulting in a lot of wasted time for Drew.

Now that we tell the client they will be charged for sketch changes beyond three, we never have the sketch process drag on. It's amazing how these little strategies are big time savers! You don't have to limit your sketches to three, like we do. Find a system that works best for you.

Save your sketches. They will be historical documents in the future, or you can sell them as artwork. We save all of Drew's sketches in a large container. We have one collector that only buys sketches. He prefers the rough sketches with Drew's notes all over them, showing the creative thought process behind the concept. After years of work, your sketches will be of historical value to you and possibly collectors.

CREATION PROCESS: Once the sketch or concept is approved by your client, you can move onto creating the art. Send your client photos as the work progresses to keep them updated. At this point, there are no more changes that can be made by the client. We make sure the client knows that their approval of the sketch is final, before the painting begins.

COMPLETION: When the work is finished, send your client a final photo and an invoice that includes sales tax and shipping (if applicable).

Tell them: "The work is complete. Once I receive final payment of $____ I will ship it to you (or email the high res to you). Payment can be sent by _____ (fill in the blank, your preference for receiving payment). Thank you!"

FOLLOW UP: A week after the art is finished, send your client a handwritten thank you note in the mail. This is old fashioned but goes a long way to further win the heart of your client. People appreciate getting a thank you note via snail mail, because of the time you took to write and send it.

SCRIPT FOR A COMMISSIONED PAINTING PROPOSAL

Below is an email script that you can use as a guide for a price quote. This script is an example that can be used for a commissioned painting, but you can use this format for any type of artwork. Change the details as needed.

Dear Joe,

Thank you for your interest in a commissioned painting. I'm very excited to create the art for you.

Below is my proposal:

Description: One commissioned painting on gallery-wrapped canvas, unframed, using acrylics as medium, sized 18"x 24", painted horizontal.

Theme: A view of Catalina Island from San Clemente, during sunset, including palm trees and the pier in the foreground.

Price: $1,800.00 plus shipping (to be determined) and 8% CA sales tax.

The price includes up to three sets of sketch changes for your approval prior to painting. (Additional sketch changes beyond the third sketch incurs a $100 per sketch fee.)

Artwork copyrights: are owned by the artist (me) and I retain all rights to reproduce the art in the future.

Payment schedule: A 50% non-refundable installment payment of $900 is required to begin the sketch process. Completed artwork will be shipped upon receipt of final payment.

Payment can be made by check (made out to _____) or by credit card or by Paypal to _____.

Timing: Allow up to two weeks for the sketch process, and once final sketch is approved by you, allow another two to three weeks for completion of the painting.

Next Step: If you are in agreement, please provide your installment payment. Upon receipt, I will begin the sketch process.

I'm looking forward to working on this for you, thank you for the opportunity. Please call me if you have any questions, at 949-555-5555.

Thanks, Jane Artist

24

QUOTING PRICES

An artist friend of mine called one day, incredibly upset. She had been working on a client's logo design for two weeks and now the client refused to pay her.

She asked me how she could get them to pay. I had two questions for her: how much did you quote, and how much of an installment payment did you get?

Her answer: she didn't get an installment payment and she never gave him a price quote. She did the work and then sent them a bill. The client responded by saying he was shocked at her price and would never pay that much for a logo.

You can see what went wrong here. The artist did the work without presenting the client with a price quote first. I don't know many people who will pay for something without first agreeing to a price. Would you? I sure wouldn't.

Every commission or project must begin with a written price quote. You don't have to type up a lengthy proposal to give a quote for most things. A price quote can be provided by email or text.

Before providing a price, have a discussion with the client on the phone, by Skype or in person. I prefer not to send price quotes by email without first personally connecting with the buyer. For many projects, there are too many variables and you need to have a complete understanding of what the client needs before you can price it out.

Also, a personal conversation helps you qualify the client as a viable client. Sometimes people like to fish for pricing by email without a real intention to buy. Asking for a phone call will weed out those time wasters.

During your conversation, ask questions to help you get a full understanding of what they want and need. The questions you should ask depend on the project. If it's about a painting commission, ask them what theme they want, what size and when do they need it.

If it's for a licensing deal, ask: "what products will the license be for" "where will they be sold" "how many images do you want to begin with" "which of my images are you most interested in" and "how many products do you plan to produce in the first run?"

If it's for an illustration or graphic design project, ask: "how many" "what's your deadline" "what is the scope of the project" "who are you targeting" and "what's the theme?" The idea is to get a full and complete understanding of their project as well as their company or personal situation.

Take notes and write down answers to their questions as you talk to them. Pay extra special attention to phrases and words they use, so that you can include them in your proposal. This shows that you listened and that you understand what they need.

As an example, one illustration client told me that they wanted Drew's illustrations to help their product appeal to boys and young men who dream of living a fun lifestyle. In my proposal under "scope of work" I included the very phrase he used.

This is a very powerful technique, one that high value providers use when writing up proposals. Clients may or may not recognize that you used their exact words, but either way, they will be impressed that you listened and understood.

It works, because in practicing it, you learn to be a better listener and you become skilled at speaking your client's language, which in turn gets you the bigger and better paying gigs.

Lastly, ask the potential client how they found you. This helps you to know where your new clients come from.

SCRIPTS:

Below is an example of an email proposal for t-shirt illustrations:

Dear Timothy,

Thank you for your interest in my artwork. This is a follow up to our conversation on the phone yesterday. You said that you want to create a line of surf wear tees under your new brand called Tidal Waves. You want it to have a touch of "edge" but not be too busy. Your target market is boys and men aged 15 to 30. The art should be either one color, two color or three color.

See below my proposal and pricing.

Description: Artist will create 8 unique designs that can be utilized for t-shirts, hats and stickers. Artwork will be slightly edgy and provided in two to three colors.

License rights are granted the client for two years, for sales in the U.S., for t-shirts, hats and stickers.

Up to three sketches per design will be provided for changes or approval. Sketch changes beyond three sketches per design will incur a $200 per sketch fee.

Finished artwork will be provided in high res PSD files. Original artwork remains in the ownership of the artist. Artist retains ownership to all copyrights.

Pricing & Fee Schedule: A one-time fee of $5,000. Additional designs beyond the initial eight will be billed separately.

A 50% installment payment is required to begin sketch work and full balance is due at completion

Timing: This will be a 6-week process from start to finish. Research and sketch work begins upon receipt of installment payment.

Next step: Send your installment payment of $2,500 via check, Paypal or credit card. I will then begin the sketch work.

Please call me with questions. I can be reached at 949-555-5555. I look forward to working with you.

Sincerely,

Joe Artist

FOLLOW UP

For every ten price quotes I give, less than half come back with a "yes." This is for many reasons, and you can never take it personally. Often, people like to fish around for information with no real intention of buying. Other times, you'll get an email from someone who really just wanted free art. And sometimes, your prices weren't in their budget. It's up to you to get to the bottom of why they didn't buy.

Follow up within 24 hours to confirm that they received your email. If they did receive it, ask "are you ready to move forward on this?"

If they hesitate or say they aren't ready, ask them why. Then sit and be quiet. Listen. They will tell you and often it's not what you think it is. Once you understand what is holding them back, you can make suggestions or find solutions to get them to decide. Strive to get either a "yes" or a "no" from them right away.

If the client says they just aren't ready yet, then say "Okay, no problem. How about I check in with you in two weeks? Does that sound good?" And then check back with them two weeks later. Email or call them. Sometimes people take a while to come around. Don't feel bad if a proposal isn't accepted. It's never personal. It's a part of doing business.

25

SELLING REPRODUCTIONS

Selling print reproductions of your work is a smart business model that enables an artist to earn money again and again from one painting. We have art that Drew painted back in the late 1990's that we are still selling reproductions of today.

When selling art at an event, it's important to have a variety of price points available to increase sales of your work, and reproductions allow for that.

As an example, your exhibit could include several original pieces in a variety of sizes that are priced between $900 - $3,000 each, while offering reproductions on paper ranging from $50 - $100 each, and reproductions on canvas ranging from $200 - $600 each.

If someone loves your work but cannot afford the original piece, they can buy a lower priced reproduction. Having various price points greatly increases your sales.

One thing that I really want artists to understand is this: you have no idea which of your art pieces will be popular, but when you stumble upon one, it will earn you revenue for decades. For this reason, it's wise to experiment with all of your images by making reproductions available and see what people like.

You will find that out of every twenty art pieces you create, one will stand out above the other nineteen as a popular image, perfect for selling reproductions. It is the popular images that successful artists earn their living from. If it's iconic enough, you will earn from it for the rest of your life.

A great example of this point is the iconic Endless Summer artwork; John Van Hamersveld created this timeless image in 1964 for The Endless Summer movie poster. Today, as I'm writing this chapter, I looked up the movie poster on EBay and signed prints of this piece are being sold for $3,000 each. At the same time, unsigned, mass reproduced posters of the artwork are being sold through numerous channels online. I'm pretty sure Van Hamersveld had no idea, in 1964, just how iconic this image would become, and that fifty years later he would still be selling prints of it. The revenues being generated by this one image are what artists dream of.

We do not have a crystal ball, so we can't possibly know which art piece will be the winner. What you love, as the artist, is usually not what everyone else loves. And vice-versa. You have to assume that any one of your pieces may become popular or iconic, and be prepared to benefit from it.

How do you prepare to benefit from your iconic artworks?

1. Ensure that you retain the copyrights (ownership) to all of your artworks.
2. Get a high res scan or digital image of all of your artwork.

3. Store all of your digital art files in an organized manner. Store them in more than one place to avoid loss. We use a combination of Dropbox, a physical hard drive and a combination hard drive and cloud product by Western Digital. Guard your digital files with your life, because it is your life's work. Once the art is gone from your studio, you often can't get it back to scan it again.

We ensure that every painting Drew creates is properly scanned and saved in a high res file before we ship the original to its new owner.

Even if we think that we won't make reproductions of a particular piece, we still capture the high res files so that we are prepared when we need an image for a printed book, magazine article or online interview by the media.

When Drew finishes a painting, before he signs it, we have it professionally shot by a photographer. This costs us $100 per image. Some people may think this is too much money to spend on a digital scan. But I consider it a cost of doing business, just like paying taxes and buying art supplies. If you plan on making a living with your art, you have to do it right.

You could shoot the image yourself if you have a good camera. We do our own for paintings sized 11" x 14" or smaller. But the larger ones require greater equipment and expertise, and we have come to learn that it's worth the money we spend to get the files done right.

We wait until after the painting is shot for Drew to sign it, so that his signature doesn't show up on print reproductions twice, as Drew will hand-sign each one. It looks strange when you have a digital signature on the reproduction and then you sign your name right next to it.

PRINTING REPRODUCTIONS

Print reproductions come in a variety of formats. You can print your art on fine paper, canvas, wood, and the new popular thing is printing art on metal.

You can print most paper prints yourself using a high quality printer and archival acid-free papers. It's a small investment but one that will allow you to print one by one, as you experiment to determine what your best sellers are.

To find someone to print your reproductions, do a search online for a local printer. Your best option will be someone who is a true artist, who understands color and who cares about quality. Some of the best printers I've worked with were actually photographers who, as a side business, printed reproductions for artists.

You can use online companies to print on canvas, such as Costco, but sometimes there is a huge problem with quality when you do that. Costco art prints look okay and are affordable, but they will not last as they don't use the best materials. Some of the online printing companies produce low quality reproductions. Be very careful about putting your art out into the world on low quality prints, because it will reflect poorly on you as the artist.

REPRODUCING COMMISSIONED WORKS

One question that I hear from artists is "Is it okay to make print reproductions of commissioned work?"

My answer is yes, if that is part of your business model. It's perfectly okay to sell print reproductions of any of your work, as long as you retain the copyrights to it and you make sure that your client is aware of it in advance.

Of course, there are always exceptions to every rule. Obviously, if you are painting a portrait or something of extreme personal nature for your client, you wouldn't make print reproductions of it. It wouldn't sell anyway.

Some collectors insist on being the only person who owns the image. In this case, you can offer the collector exclusive rights to the commissioned art for an increase in price. Most artists charge three or four times the price of the original for exclusive rights. Of course, most collectors are not willing to pay extra for exclusivity.

We have created an entire business from reproducing Drew's art. This business model has sustained us through lean years, as not everyone can afford an original.

Drew created a painting called *Deep into Paradise* for a collector a few years ago. Recently we decided to release a limited edition, signed and numbered canvas reproduction of the work, and it has surprisingly become one of our most popular images. We sold over a dozen of the canvas prints in the first day of releasing it. This is great for the owner of the original, as the value of his piece has increased. He's the only one with the original!

The next question in your mind may be this: "But won't your buyer of the original be upset if their art is reproduced?"

It depends on who your collectors are. If you are only selling in premium galleries and your pieces are going for over $30,000 each, maybe it will be an issue with the gallery owners. Or if you're painting portraits, you shouldn't reproduce something that personal. But for most artists who are reading this, it will be entirely okay for you to adopt this business model.

I've only had one person, out of almost twenty years of selling Drew's art, question this practice. It was a gallery owner in Laguna Beach, who insisted that Drew's collectors won't appreciate seeing their painting on reproductions. I worried he might be right. So I spent a few days cold calling over fifty of Drew's collectors.

I asked them one question: "As an owner of one of Drew's original paintings, would it bother you to see the art reproduced?"

It was surprising the positive responses I got. One collector said, "I saw my Drew painting on a skimboard in Florida last summer and I was so happy! I have the original hanging in my home."

Every single person I asked said that it would be okay, and most expressed pride at owning the original piece of art. Except for one guy; he was the last phone call I made. He said he wanted the art all to himself and would be angry to find that it had been reproduced. After I explained to him the business model and how it would increase the value of his painting, he changed his feelings about it.

What I learned from that exercise was this—Drew's collectors understand how Drew works with art and they love being a part of the story. They respect our business model, as we have "trained" people to know what to expect. It's important to us to keep our collectors happy and we have life-long relationships with many of them.

Our *business model* is to sell art print reproductions on paper or canvas, and/or license the work, of any of the paintings that Drew creates. Only you, the artist, can decide what model you want to use for your business.

Your collectors can't dictate your business model, no more than you can dictate what they do with their business. It's up to you to decide *how* you will run your own business. If you decide that this isn't the best course of action for the type of art that you create, then don't do it. But, if you feel that it works well for the type of work you do, go for it.

I have found that 99% of the people in the world will respect your business model, when it's clearly defined.

26

NEGOTIATING

Being raised in a small town in America, where everyone is friendly, negotiating felt like an unfriendly thing to do. I was taught to be nice, to give in and to do what others wanted. I believed that to be good at negotiating, it meant that you had to be unfair and take more than you give.

After being in business and putting deals together for so many years, I've come to learn that wasn't true. A good negotiator doesn't screw the other person over; they simply find a way to work things out in a positive way. A good negotiation is one where both parties are happy in the end.

When it comes to survival in business, I've had to teach myself how to negotiate. I read many books on the subject and I've taken negotiating workshops through Karrass, Inc. It helped.

Anyone can learn how to negotiate. It takes a little bit of knowledge and a lot of practice. It also takes the proper mindset. Rather than viewing negotiating as a negative, see it instead as a way of compromising so that both parties get the most important things that they want.

When you negotiate with a client, that should be your goal; a good deal for both parties. If one party will be unhappy, you haven't done your job. If it's impossible to make both parties happy, then the deal shouldn't go through.

Below are basic strategies and guidelines that you can use when negotiating, which will help prevent you from making a big mistake in your next business deal.

BE PATIENT

This is the most important negotiating tip you'll ever hear. Do not respond to a request or offer until after you have had time to think about it. Never agree to anything on the spot. When someone offers you something, tell them you'll give it some thought and respond to them shortly.

Then, take time to think. Consider all aspects of what you are being offered and of what you would like to ask for. Take time to ask questions and gain greater understanding before giving a response.

If you agree too quickly, you may forget something important and regret it later.

YOU DON'T HAVE TO GIVE
EVERYTHING THEY ASK FOR

An artist called me about a licensing contract he was about to sign with a wall art company. They were offering him a $500 up front advance and 9% in royalties. Their contract was well written and very fair to the artist, except for one thing. They wanted 150 of his images. The artist did not want to give them that much art, not yet. It was part of his business model to reserve certain images for limited edition prints only.

I recommended he tell the wall art company that he is willing to provide them with the images that he's releasing for open edition, and that some of the images will be reserved for limited edition. The limited edition images will not be a part of their contract.

The artist worried that by making this demand, he would lose the deal. But that wasn't what happened; the company respected his business model and agreed to take the images he was willing to give them. They were okay with him holding back the ones that he deemed limited edition.

Some clients will ask for things you don't want to give. It's because they don't know your business model or future plans. How could they? It's up to you to let them know what you are willing to give and what you are not willing to give.

BE FIRM AND SOUND CONFIDENT

When you firmly tell your client what you can and cannot do, you are taking control of your business and earning their respect at the same time.

Use phrases such as "I don't do xxx, but I will do yyy instead. Does that work for you?"

When a client asks us to sign a "work for hire" agreement, I'll say "We don't do work for hire. But what I can do is give you limited rights to use the art for what you need it for. Fair enough?"

When you say "I don't do ...," you are announcing to your client a very firm stance. Most people will respect that and look for another way to get what they need. But if you say "Well, um, I don't know about that..." the client will push you to do it.

Never waiver on your response to your clients. If you sound wishy washy, they will try to convince you to do something you don't want to do, and if you cave in, you'll regret it later. Stay firm, friendly and confident.

NEGOTIATING MUSTS

RESEARCH: Research as much as you can about the company and the people you are dealing with. Look up their most recent campaign or products. Get a feel for what is important to them and their branding. Come to understand who they are as a brand and a company so that you can learn what is important to them. This will aid in your negotiation.

KNOW WHAT YOU WANT: Know specifically what you want before entering into any negotiation. If you don't know what you want, you'll never get it. Write down on a piece of paper three things:

1. Your desired outcome; be very specific and make a list that includes pricing, timing and details such as how

you will be marketing, how your art will be printed, and what you want overall.

2. The lowest outcome that you will agree to if you have to; and

3. Your deal breaker, which is the outcome that will cause you to walk away from the deal.

ASK QUESTIONS: Be aware that everyone wants something. What does your client want? What do they need? What is important to them? What are they afraid of?

One of our clients chose another artist over Drew for a major campaign illustration job, as his price was lower than ours. They paid him a deposit and shortly after, the artist disappeared without delivering the work. This client now had two problems; they were up against a tight deadline, and they had just been screwed over and lost their money. After losing two weeks on the project, they came back to us for a revised quote and asked us to lower our price. We refused and instead, we addressed what they really wanted. We convinced them that it was worth paying for an artist who will deliver by deadline and help them avoid a disaster. Their fear was that if they were to go to another unreliable, but cheaper artist, they would find themselves right back where they were, without the art they needed. In the end, they agreed to our price.

Ask questions. Talk less, Listen More. Dig deep with your questions so that you know what their concerns are and their needs are. Sometimes it's not what you think.

Some of the questions you can ask clients to get into their head:

"What do you feel is the most important outcome of this project?"

"What problems have you had in the past with these types of projects?"

"What is it that you like about my work?"

"Who else have you asked for a proposal/price quote?"

"What other artists have you worked with? How was your experience with them?"

"What is the biggest concern you have about this?"

ASK FOR WHAT YOU WANT: Many artists hesitate to ask for something extra, fearing they will lose the deal. No one is going to withdraw their interest in you just because you asked for something.

Always ask for what you want. The worst thing they can do is say no. Often, a client will pay or give more than you expect. Most of your clients will want you to be happy.

Some of the things I've asked for, and got: plane tickets and hotel rooms, free art supplies, travel fees, merchandise and free advertising.

DON'T GIVE UNLESS YOU GET: Concessions should be tit for tat. A concession is something that is removed from the deal or added to the deal. For example, if the client asks you to lower your price then you should lessen the scope of work. Or if they ask for more work than you quoted for, add to the price.

Never grant a concession without anything given to you in return. Make sure that if the other party asks you to make a concession, that you are given something extra. In business deals, you can get very creative with this. Ask for free advertising or extra products or plane tickets.

BE FLEXIBLE: Don't be afraid to change your offer if they change the details. Make creative adjustments to your offer to fit their budget or their situation.

Often we are wary of changing our offer in the middle of the game. But sometimes it's necessary, especially when the deal has changed and new information is gained during discussions. Don't be afraid to withdraw something you offered earlier, if it makes sense to do so now.

BRAINSTORM AND GET CREATIVE: Brainstorm creative ideas to make the deal fair to everyone. Business author Seth Godin said "The best deals are ones that have never been done before." This is absolutely true in the business of art. Most of the deals I put together have been creatively crafted by myself and the client.

FOLLOW UP WITH WRITTEN DOCUMENTATION: Follow all of your conversations and negotiations with a written recap. Craft an email to your client, detailing what you agreed to. This will ensure that you both have clarity on what was discussed and there can be no disagreements about it later.

NEGOTIATING NO-NO's

Never negotiate against yourself. If you gave an offer or a price and the other person didn't accept it, DO NOT offer them a lower number. This is called negotiating against yourself. Instead, ask them to make you a counter-offer.

Don't fall for the "hurry up and sign" gambit. If your client is in a giant hurry to get you started on the art, get them to slow down long enough to nail down the agreement between the two of you. For some people, "hurry up and sign" or "hurry up and get started" ends up in a disaster for the artist. They either don't get paid, or they are pushed into agreeing to a bad deal.

We once had a client tell us they needed a three week project in less than ten days. We agreed to a price and I told them we required an installment payment to get Drew started on the sketches. They moved surprisingly slow for someone who was in a rush; I suppose they didn't believe me. Three days went by and no payment. Now we were down to seven days for Drew to do the work. I called and told them if they wanted Drew to start on the sketches, they would have to get us the installment payment asap. If he didn't get started he wouldn't be able to meet their tight deadline. I used their rush to our advantage. They bank wired the payment immediately.

Sometimes a client will rush you to sign a contract before you have time to think about what you are agreeing to. Never do this! Slow things down. Make it clear that you need time to read through their contract and understand it. If you don't agree to something in the contract, have them change it. If they are in a hurry, they will move quickly to make the changes you request. When a client is in a big hurry, it's actually to your advantage. You hold all the power, as they need you to move fast.

Never agree to a deal that you don't fully understand or that is vague and confusing. Correct this by writing out what you do understand and then outlining your questions to your client. Get clarity by asking your client to explain those points that you don't understand. Do not feel bad about asking questions; it's a poor reflection on you if you don't get clarity on everything.

Never try to negotiate with someone who doesn't make the decisions. If the person you're dealing with says "I have to go ask my boss now if he agrees", insist that you deal directly with the person making the decisions. Don't fall for this game. It's a negotiating tactic.

Don't fall for the, "but it's great promotion for you" line. When negotiating a business deal, the price you are paid should have absolutely nothing to do with how well the product will sell or how many famous people are involved or anything else that is irrelevant. When a client uses this line, ignore it.

If the deal feels bad or turns your stomach, don't agree to it. Don't be afraid to walk away. You are not obligated to agree to something you don't want. A bad deal is a bad deal.

27

PAYMENT POLICIES

Every good business has an established payment policy. Yours should, too. Having a strict payment policy, communicating it clearly and sticking to it, will avoid misunderstandings with clients.

Three powerful payment policies that keep us in business are:

1. For commissions and projects we require a 50% installment payment to begin the work and the final balance is due on the day of completion.
2. For existing artwork and products, payment is required in full at the time of purchase.
3. For existing artworks priced over $2,000, we offer payment plans.

Having an established payment policy avoids the possibility of being stiffed on payment, which is something that happens to every artist at least once. If it has never happened to you, you have either been lucky or you are a very savvy business person.

I have talked to scores of artists who have complained that a client disappeared without paying, after the artist provided the art. This never happens when you have a good policy in place.

The most effective payment policy is simple and it works beautifully: A 50% installment payment is due up front, before you start the work, and the full balance is due upon completion of the work.

For digital art, we send the client low res files to see the finished product, and then we send the high res files upon receipt of final payment. For tangible artwork, we ship or deliver the work after payment is made. For wall murals and live events, we require final payment on the day of completion.

This policy enables us to move quickly from one project to the next. Receiving final payment signals us to provide the artwork, and then the project is complete. Once a project is done and paid for, we can move onto the next one. I don't ever want to have to worry about getting payment later, after the fact.

When dealing with companies overseas, I require payment by bank wire transfer. A bank wire transfer is a standard method of payment for overseas transactions and the main benefit of it is that it cannot easily be reversed or refunded. An international bank wire transfer will cost you, the receiver, a bank wire fee of about $25-$60, depending on your bank. Keep this in mind when invoicing your client, so you can add a bank wire fee to their invoice.

I am very careful not to send art or high res files to an overseas client until after payment is made. If you are not paid properly by a company overseas, it is incredibly difficult to track them down for payment. A bank wire transfer can take three to five days to show up in your bank account, so if the client is on a tight deadline, they may need to pay extra to their bank to have your wire payment expedited.

My second best payment option for overseas would be Paypal, as it is instantly received in your Paypal account with little to no wait time. However, a Paypal payment can be disputed by the client later.

Your payment policy should be clearly communicated to your client in the first conversation, when you are discussing their project. One way to communicate this is to say, "I'm excited to work with you. This is how I work; once I have an understanding of what you need, I will send you a price quote. I will need a 50% installment payment to get started." Your proposal, price quote or agreement will include the details of your payment policy.

When an individual collector commissions Drew for an original painting, we require a 50% installment payment before Drew begins the sketch work. We send the client photo updates of the work in progress, and when it's complete, we ask for final payment before shipping the work to them.

When doing wall mural projects, we require 50% to schedule the date and buy the supplies, and then the final balance on the day the mural is completed. We don't leave the mural site until after we are paid. We make sure the client knows to expect this, and we remind them days in advance to have our payment ready. I have never had a problem being paid for a mural project on the last day of painting, as I have communicated my expectations to the client many times during the process.

When working with companies for illustration work, we handle it in a similar way. The client is updated of progress along the way, and once the work is complete, we send them low res images to view. We send the final, high res files to the client after they have paid in full.

Our proposals with companies include a pricing section that reads like this:

PRICING AND PAYMENT: $6,000 total. A 50% installment payment of $3,000 is required to begin the work. Final balance is due and payable upon completion, and no later than ten days following completed date. Artwork will be provided upon receipt of final payment. Late payments incur late fee of $25 each week that payment is not received.

MONEY IS A COMMITMENT

Paying money up front equals commitment by the client. Once we receive their commitment in the form of a payment, we add their project to Drew's schedule and we commit our time and materials as necessary. The installment payment is our "green light" to move forward on their project.

We didn't always work this way, though. We learned the hard way. When I first started working with Drew, I was inconsistent with my payment policies. I would not always require an installment up front and sometimes I would deliver the art without final payment. Eventually, I realized that I was wasting a lot of time making phone calls to clients asking for payment. Most people eventually paid, but it added a lot of stress on me to chase the money down.

Then, one incident happened that changed the way we worked with clients forever. Drew was commissioned by a very large clothing company. They hired him to create an artistic map of one of the Hawaiian Islands. The art was going to be used for apparel and accessories. They were on an incredibly tight deadline and needed it yesterday. We felt that there was no time to get an installment payment from them, it was such a rush. If I knew then what I know now, I would have told them to overnight the payment to get Drew started on the sketches. But we were young and inexperienced! Drew began the work without any payment. He put in three days of drawing up sketches for them as the art director at the company kept making changes and asking him to revise it. Then, the art director stopped calling. They had changed their campaign and decided not to use a map after all. We sent them an invoice for the work Drew did for them, and they never paid us. I made numerous phone calls trying to get paid, and hit a brick wall every time. It's nearly impossible to be paid after the fact by a large company.

I was incredibly upset; we just lost two thirds of our income for that week. Our son was a baby at the time and cash flow was crucial to paying our expenses. Losing three days of pay was a financial strain on us. I vowed that it would never happen again.

We learned from our mistake, and since then have required 50% up front and the balance when finished. We use this policy on everyone, even friends and family members.

Some artists are uncomfortable asking for an installment payment. They fear that the client thinks they don't trust them. But there is more to it than trust. The installment money generates cash flow, which enables you to put the proper amount of time and materials into the beginning phase of a project.

Most of our commissions take two to three weeks to complete. Without an installment payment, we would not have the cash flow we need to pay for daily expenses or to cover the cost of the canvas and paint.

The installment payment is a promise from your client that they are committed to the project, enough so that you should put your money and time into it.

HOW MUCH OF AN INSTALLMENT SHOULD YOU ASK FOR?

Many artists require 50% up front. Some artists require 30% up front.

For larger deals, you may want to break the payments into three equal payments. For example, we just closed an $18,000 illustration deal with a company that we had never worked with before. They have had trouble with this project in the past, as they had numerous artists work on it but none were able to produce what they wanted. To allow them to try out Drew's concepts in the form of sketches first, we formulated a different payment plan that allowed them to not continue should they not be pleased with the sketches we provide. In our written proposal and agreement we divided the $18,000 into three payments. The first installment is $6,000 to get Drew started on sketches. If they are happy with Drew's concepts, then they will pay another $6,000 to move onto the next phase, creating the illustrations. Lastly, once the illustrations are complete, they will send the final $6,000 and we will then send them the high res files.

INSTALLMENT PAYMENTS ARE NON-REFUNDABLE

Installment payments should be considered non-refundable. The main reason for the installment payment is to cover your initial material expenses and time. If the client pulls out, disappears or changes their mind after you invested time and money, they lose their installment payment.

HOW DO YOU ASK FOR AN INSTALLMENT PAYMENT?

In every conversation with a new client, we mention (even with friends, acquaintances and relatives) that we need an installment payment to get started.

You may feel strange asking for this. Don't worry, it will come naturally to you over time. When giving a price quote, include your installment requirement in writing by e-mail or proposal.

Over time, your returning customers will know what you expect and they will be prepared to give you payment for the up front for future projects. All of our longtime customers are familiar with the way we work. They also know that the work will be done to their satisfaction, because they've worked with us before.

WHAT IF THERE IS RESISTANCE TO PAYING AN INSTALLMENT?

Sometimes it's the artists themselves who hesitate to require an installment payment from their client. They feel desperate for the work and are afraid to sound demanding.

Here's a perspective I want you to consider; if you are desperate for work, then you surely cannot afford to spend time on something that you might never get paid for.

In the art business, it's very common for artists to be stiffed of payment. The scenario always goes like this: an artist is approached by someone who loves their work and asks the artist to create for them. The artist gets excited and forgets to price it properly or get an installment payment. They do the work and then ask for payment; the client never intended to pay that much, or decided they didn't want it. The artist is now financially harmed and upset.

Requiring an installment payment avoids that scenario by weeding out the payers from the non-payers. The people who most likely will never pay you are the ones who won't pay money up front. The people willing to pay up front are the ones that are serious.

It's very rare for me to have a client that doesn't want to pay an installment up front. But every now and again I get some resistance. Below are some tips on how to handle it.

WHEN THE CLIENT REFUSES TO PAY AN INSTALLMENT

If a client refuses to pay an installment, sometimes it means that they just aren't ready to commit. If that's the case, then you shouldn't commit your time to their project until they are ready.

Don't feel upset when this happens. Be graceful and let them know that you are happy to start the work after they pay. Tell them to call you when they are ready. Be friendly and professional.

There are other reasons a client might not pay an installment, listed below.

WHEN THEY DON'T HAVE THE MONEY

I've run into this many times. When I tell someone that they have to pay 50% up front, and then they say "Oh, I don't have the money right now," this tells me that it's possible they may never have it. So I say "When you do, let me know. We are looking forward to working with you."

WHEN YOU ARE NEW AT YOUR CRAFT

If you've been at your craft for less than 2 years, you may still have to prove yourself before you can require 50% up front. Maybe the client isn't sure of your abilities and they are nervous to invest in you. In this case, lower the amount you ask for to 20% instead. This way, you still get the benefit of the client making a commitment, and the client gets the benefit of a lower financial risk.

WHEN THE CLIENT IS IN A HURRY FOR YOU TO GET STARTED AND THERE IS NO TIME TO PAY YOU RIGHT NOW

If the client is in a hurry, they will hurry up and send the money so that you can get started. Stick to your guns, don't give in. You hold all the power when they are rushed with a deadline. Use it to your advantage and suggest they either pay by Paypal, credit card or Overnight Express you a check. Don't start the work without the installment payment.

WHEN YOUR CLIENT IS A HUGE 5 BILLION DOLLAR COMPANY AND THEY TAKE 3 WEEKS TO CUT CHECKS

BUT THEY NEED YOU TO GET THE WORK DONE BY FRIDAY

I've been faced with this scenario many, many times. Here's what I do: I ask the client to write me a personal check or credit card and they can bill their company for it later. The serious ones send me their personal check or credit card. Others suddenly are able to get their company to cut a check quickly. There is always a way to be paid up front, even with large companies.

If you absolutely cannot get an installment payment from a large company, then a signed contract or legally binding purchase order, issued by the company's purchasing department, would be your next best option.

THEY AREN'T CONVINCED YOU CAN DO THE WORK

This is a valid concern if the artist is newly out of school and just getting started. However, if you have been at your craft for more than three years, and you have a lot of happy clients, this is an easy problem to solve. Show your new client past projects that you have done. Provide references that the client can call if they doubt your abilities. Put them at ease. Once they are confident you can do what they need, they will happily pay your installment.

THEY FLAT OUT REFUSE

If they just refuse to make a payment up front, take the time to find out why, and put their concerns at ease. If it's because they can't afford it, then they aren't a viable client and you'll have to move on.

If there is no good reason for them to refuse, it's possible you'll never get paid by them, no matter what you do, because of a lack of commitment on their part. In this case, walk away. You'll save yourself a lot of wasted time and frustration.

Some clients are high maintenance and difficult to do business with. The people that demand cheaper rates and avoid paying installments are typically the same people who will give you the hardest time during a project. You don't have to take on every client. It's okay to say "no" to clients that will be disrespectful and difficult.

EXCEPTIONS AND BEING FLEXIBLE TO THE 50% INSTALLMENT PAYMENT RULE

There are exceptions to every rule. In the many years I've been using this process, I've only made a few. One was when we did a deal with Converse Shoes and it took them six weeks to get us a check. However, we had a contract in writing and they had advised me in advance that it would take that long to be paid. It was a huge deal for us, so we were flexible.

When a project requires a lot of money and time on our end, I can't afford to be flexible on the installment, because in doing so, it would harm our business. We once did a big project with Western Digital, our largest client to date. The project was huge, and just our cost of materials was over $4,000 out of pocket. My contact there told me that it took thirty to ninety days to get paid through their accounting system. I explained that we don't have the cash flow to front the cost of expenses, plus the month of time it would take Drew to do the artwork. I had a lengthy conversation with my client, explaining that we are a small business, and by waiting 90 days to get paid, it would put a great strain on us. He took our concerns into consideration, and was able to get his accounting department to issue a payment quickly.

When there is a lot of time involved on our end, I'm not willing to take on the project without an adequate installment payment. A few years ago, a large shoe company approached us to do a complete line of Drew Brophy flip flops. We had many meetings with them and they were excited to get started. Drew was going to create all new artwork for the line, which would have been about four full weeks of work.

We asked them for an advance payment up front, to cover the time Drew would be committing. They were up against a tight deadline and pushed him to get started immediately. But no check came. A week went by. I finally called, saying "Drew is eager to get started. But we haven't received the check." They said it was coming. It never came. They disappeared. I was shocked, because our meetings went so well and we had the entire line planned out. When it came to putting money down, they were not committed to the project. I'm grateful that we didn't block off a month of Drew's time for nothing.

One way artists get themselves into deep financial distress is by working on non-paying projects for people who aren't committed to it. When people express amazement at the fact that Drew and I have been able to make a good living off of

Drew's artwork, I tell them that these are some of the strategies that I attribute our success to.

Being consistent with payment policies and *not allowing others to drain our business financially* are the sound practices that enable us to succeed.

HOW TO RAISE YOUR PRICES

An artist wrote me: "I have been in this business a long time and I have a degree. But I struggle with getting paid what I want for designs. I hear excuses like 'I give you consistent work' or 'we are just a new company'. I've been told that I am easy to work with and my designs sell well. So it confuses me when I ask to be paid more and they don't think I deserve an increase. It's hard to stick up for myself even though I am confident the work is good quality."

This artist is making the mistake of allowing his clients to dictate his pricing. This is an easy problem to fix. He is educated, experienced and his designs have a history of selling well. It would be risky for a client to stop working with him and give another artist a chance, because there are so many artists out there that are not good at what they do.

The problem is not his client, but how he has trained them to think of him. Charging reasonable prices is not "sticking up for yourself." It's operating your business properly.

The way to set this right is to change the way you communicate with your clients. From this point forward, your prices are not negotiable, they are what they are. Just like your attorney's prices are set and your gas prices are set and the prices at the grocery store are set.

If you have been under-charging your clients, raise your prices immediately. Do this by properly communicating with them. Send a letter to all of your clients that states:

"Effective immediately my prices have increased by 20%. I value my relationship with you and want to give you my best work possible. This minor adjustment will allow me to continue to give you the excellent service I have been, while being able to run my business properly. Please let me know if you have any questions."

When you make a decision and an announcement, no one will argue with you. If they do argue, tell them, "I'm sorry, the decision has been made. I do hope you value my work and continue to work with me, as you are an important client and friend."

CHARGE FOR EXTRAS

Always charge your client for additional expenses and services. Many artists make the mistake of eating extra costs. They will say things like "oh, it's only $20, I'll just pay for it" or "a digital file costs me nothing, I won't charge them extra." But your time and expenses add up and reduce your overall income. If your client requests something extra, or there are additional expenses out of your pocket, charge them for it.

Below are examples of line items that freelancers should charge extra for. Some artists include the prices in either the proposal as an additional line item, or they include it in the overall price. Regardless, make sure your client pays for the extras.

- Embellishment
- Added materials, increase in complexity of project, additional fees due to client's unexpected changes
- Rush Fee
- Extra revisions to sketches beyond a set number
- Reproduction rights
- Credit card or Paypal processing fees
- Bank wire fees
- Digital files to replace files that the client lost
- Project files (in graphic design)
- Any changes that the client makes to the original scope of work
- Shipping costs
- Boxing and packaging costs
- Sales tax
- Delivery Fees
- Travel expenses, hotel, lodging

KILL FEES

A "Kill Fee" can be added to your agreements for extra protection. It is an amount the artist would be paid if the project is "killed" or canceled by the client before it's complete. This protects against you doing all the work, only to have your client say "sorry, we changed our minds." A kill fee is typically used by illustrators, but can be worked into any type of deal.

Kill fees range from 50% to 100% of the cost of the entire project. Many artists charge a 75% kill fee. If you had received 50% up front as an installment payment, your kill fee would be an additional 25%. An example:

PRICING AND PAYMENT: $3,000 total. A 50% installment payment of $1,500 is required to begin the sketch process. Final balance is due and payable to the artist at completion. An additional kill fee of $750 is payable to the artist should the project be canceled or discontinued by the Client. The kill fee is due immediately upon cancellation.

For very large projects, your kill fee may be structured to have different amounts for cancellation at different stages in the project. At the halfway stage of the project, the kill fee may be 75% of the total price. At the two thirds stage of the project, your kill fee may be 100%. You can decide what works best for you and your client.

28

COPYRIGHTS

"When you sign your copyrights away,
you are giving up future earning potential."
—Maria Brophy

Often I am asked if an artist should sell all of their copyrights to a client. Most of the time, my answer is "no." If you are an artist who visualizes long term success with your art, you must be in control of all of your artwork. Your art is your brand and you must protect it.

Of course, as with everything in the art business, there are a few exceptions to this, such as graphic logo design or if it is your business model as an illustrator to transfer copyrights to your client.

When Drew was 25 years old, he received the best piece of advice that set the course for his future success as an artist. At the time, he was painting surfboards and designing t-shirts for surf companies. He knew very little about the business of art.

He never thought about things like copyrights or ownership of his images.

Then Drew met art agent Gordon McClelland. Gordon had previously represented the late, great Rick Griffin, a California artist famously known for his psychedelic poster art for bands such as the Grateful Dead and Bob Dylan, and Zap Comix art from back in the 60's and 70's. Rick Griffin's work was a huge inspiration to Drew.

If Drew was destined to become a well-known artist, then meeting Gordon McClelland was an act of fate. Gordon uttered a warning that set the course for Drew's future success. He said, "Drew, don't ever sign your copyrights away to anyone."

Drew didn't understand how copyrights worked at the time. But he listened as Gordon explained that the art he was creating now could earn him money for years to come, and that later it could be passed onto his children, if he kept ownership of it. Gordon also explained how licensing worked, and how Drew could earn money again and again off of one image.

Drew took Gordon's advice, and from that day forward, on his hand-written invoices to his clients, Drew added a line that read "Artist retains all copyrights."

Thanks to Gordon's advice, Drew owns all of the art images he ever created. Since then, we have earned money again and again off of Drew's most popular images.

There are two very sound business reasons to own your copyrights:

1. It allows you to control where your art ends up. You decide how it is sold and how it is portrayed to the world.

When you sign your rights away, the new owner of your copyrights can do anything they want with your art, even things that would harm your brand or go against your personal values. For an artist with a distinctive style, this could negatively impact your brand as an artist and make your fans angry. An example would be that of a fine artist who signs their rights away and later finds their work being printed on poor quality items sold in bargain basement stores.

2. It allows you to earn money from your art again and again. You can leverage your time by earning money from licensing, merchandising and reproductions. Your library of images will be passed down to your family and your children will earn from it long after you're gone.

When you sign your copyrights away, you give up future earning potential. In other words, it takes money out of your pocket and gives it to someone else. This is why musicians don't usually sell the rights to their songs. When they stumble on a hit song, they can earn from it over and over again.

One of Drew's images, titled *Pure Joy*, was painted in 2001. The original painting was sold at an art gallery in Laguna Beach, California. It was a small painting on canvas and it sold for $450 to a collector from Los Angeles. The image itself became iconic in surf culture and has been printed on everything from magazine covers to art prints to apparel and hard goods. To date, *Pure Joy* has earned us well over $250,000 in licensing and reproduction sales. Just think, if we had only sold the original of *Pure Joy* for $450 and didn't keep the copyrights, we would have earned only $450 from it instead of $250,000.

Did we have a crystal ball that told us *Pure Joy* would have that kind of earning power? Well, we knew it was one of Drew's better paintings, but there was no way of knowing that it would become as popular as it did. This is why we scan and capture the image of everything Drew creates, even commissioned work that he does for his clients; any one of them could end up being an iconic image with immense earning power.

When a collector commissions an art piece, they pay for the painting and they own the rights to hang it on their wall. We retain the rights to reproduce it in any way we wish.

One exception to this rule of keeping ownership to artwork is when creating graphic design work for a company, in the form of a logo or other intellectual property that is owned by the client. The client must own rights to their own logo and branding for obvious reasons.

Another exception is when illustrators are hired to create work that includes their client's intellectual property, for example, movie posters or work you would do for Disney. Of course, in that case, the client has to retain the copyrights.

HOW COPYRIGHTS WORK

In the U.S., every artistic expression is protected by copyright law. A painting, sculpture, poem, book and song is considered intellectual property, which is owned by someone, usually the creator.

The person or entity who owns the copyright to an artwork has all legal rights to determine what happens with that artwork, including how it will be reproduced, where it will be sold and how it will be modified.

If you sign your copyrights away, and later you want to print a coffee table book of your art, or put photos of your art online, you have to get permission from each and every owner of your work.

When you sign your copyrights away, the owner of your art now can do anything they want with it. You could walk into Walmart one day and see your art as one of the POP displays. Or, it could end up on a porn site or somewhere else that goes against your personal values and dreams.

Some artists regularly sign their rights away to their clients. At times this may be okay for illustrators to do. But fine artists and artists who are building a brand and a name with their art for the long term, should make it their business model to keep ownership to their copyrights.

In the United States, the copyright owner has all reproduction rights to the art, including printing, advertising and licensing. No one else can legally reproduce, print or use art in any way without the copyright owner's written consent, not even someone who bought the original piece of art.

From the moment you create an original piece of art, you own the copyright to it. You own the copyright even if you did not legally file for copyright protection through the U.S. Copyright office.

A few exceptions to the rule above: If you created the art for an employer, then they own it. If you collaborated with another artist, then it is jointly owned. If you signed away or transferred your rights to another person or company in a written agreement, then they own it.

HOW TO PROTECT YOUR COPYRIGHTS

Don't sign any document with a client that includes language that transfers your copyrights. Beware of any language that uses words or phrases such as "Work for Hire" or "Transfer of Copyrights" or "Transfer of Rights." If a client asks you to sign a document that includes any indication of a transfer of rights, ask them to remove the language and replace it with this: "Artist retains all copyrights to the artwork."

To best protect your copyrights, you should file copyrights for all of your artwork. Every country has their own process. In the United States, you can file online at www.copyright.gov. Filing will give you the most protection in the event someone infringes upon your work illegally.

An example of copyright infringement is when someone takes your art and prints it on a product and then sells it commercially. This happens often to artists, and it's very frustrating.

When you file your copyrights, you have more legal protection. If you sue an infringer and you win the lawsuit, you'll receive greater compensation and your attorney's fees will be reimbursed. Without filing for your copyrights, legal fees are your responsibility when suing, and even if you win in court, your legal fees will often be too high to make it worthwhile pursuing.

WHEN IS IT OKAY TO SIGN COPYRIGHTS AWAY TO A CLIENT?

Illustrators and artists often come across clients who want to own all rights to the art. Sometimes the clients have good reason, other times they don't know why they want all rights, they just think they need them, but they don't.

If the artwork directly includes the client's logo, branding or intellectual property, then you will have to allow them to own copyrights because they are going to have to use their logo and branding forever.

If the artwork is a co-branding of the client's logo or branding, you can retain rights to the artwork, just not their logo or branding. (For example: Your art is printed on Absolut Vodka's labels—they don't get the rights to your art, you don't get the rights to their logo. Each party keeps ownership of their own copyrights.)

Below is my test to help you determine if you should sign your copyrights away as a business model:

An artist *should not* sign away their copyrights to a client, if:

- The artist has a distinct style that is easily recognized

- The artist plans to become well-known or famous for their art
- The artist's business model includes future art licensing and selling merchandise with their work
- The artist's goal is to build their art business based on their name and art

Signing your rights away will compromise all of these goals.

An artist may sign their rights away, if:

- The artist does not have a distinct style (their work is not recognized as their own)
- The artist does not care to become known for their art
- The artist's business model is to sign away rights
- The artist's future goals will not be compromised by it

When you give up all rights to an image, you give up all possibility of future earnings for your art. As such, you must charge more than an artist who does not sign their rights away.

The standard practice in the business of illustration is to have two prices; a price for creation of the artwork which gives the client rights to use it, and a second option that charges the client three to four times more for all rights.

HOW TO HANDLE A CLIENT WHO DEMANDS TO OWN THE COPYRIGHTS

It's not uncommon to have a client want to own copyrights to Drew's art. When this happens, I take the time to explain that our business model is to retain the copyrights. And then I have a conversation to find out why they feel they need to own the art. In the end, I can get them to agree to a limited license.

One year the surf company Billabong commissioned Drew to paint a surfboard that was going to be displayed in one of their stores. When I sent them an invoice, they sent me a "work for hire" contract to sign. They said this was required to be signed before they could pay the invoice. "Work for hire" means that the rights are being transferred from you, the artist, to the client. Of course, we weren't going to sign it. It doesn't fit in with our business model. So, I called the client and asked why they needed to own all copyrights to the surfboard art by Drew. She didn't know. I took the time to explain that we don't transfer copyrights, ever. After a lengthy conversation, she got the approval from her legal department and removed the requirement to sign the Work for Hire agreement.

Many times, I find that the company asking to own the copyrights doesn't really need to; they are asking to because they don't know how the art business works. They may want to own the art because they think they are supposed to, or because they are afraid that by not owning it, it will harm them.

This is why conversation is so important. I will ask them questions, such as "what are your real concerns" or "what are you worried about" or "what do you plan to do with the artwork that requires you to own it forever?"

Through this conversation, it often is revealed that they are worried about something that can be easily remedied without transferring copyrights. For example, we did a deal with a skateboard company many years ago, and they wanted to own the art. I asked why, and they said that they didn't want to see this particular art on any other skateboards in the marketplace. To remedy their concern, I put it in the contract that the images we were licensing to them would not be used for any other skateboard company during the term of the contract. They were happy with that and we closed the deal.

Once a clothing company wanted to own all rights to t-shirt designs that Drew was going to create for them. I asked them how long they planned to sell these t-shirts, and they said for a season, which is about four months. They only needed rights to use the artwork for a season, not forever and ever.

Sometimes a client will say that they don't want to see the art on any other product, ever. That's when I have to explain to them how our business model works, and how by printing the art on other products, it actually increases the sales of their products. For example, if an image is printed on canvas prints and it becomes a popular image, and then you take that image and print it on a product such as cell phone covers, the cell phone covers will sell better because the public has seen the image before and the public tends to buy what they are familiar with.

Most of the time, your client doesn't need all rights; most will need the art for a short period of time (a season, a year, two years). Instead of signing your rights away, offer to license the art to them for a short period of time. And stand your ground on this, because your art career depends on it.

HOW TO ORGANIZE YOUR COPYRIGHT FILINGS

If you haven't registered your copyrights in the past, don't despair. It's not too late to start. If your art is out there in the world, begin the process today.

If you have artwork that you created this month, register that artwork today. Worry about past artworks later, just get started with your most recent work first.

To register your copyrights in the U.S., go to www.copyright.gov and set up an account. This is where you will do your online copyright registrations. I'm not going to sugar coat it; the U.S. Copyright Office has made it a little confusing. But after you file a few times, you'll get the hang of it.

The U.S. copyright.gov website has an excellent section of "frequently asked questions" that you can refer to. The information is actually easy to read and understand for most of us without a law degree.

Put yourself on a system of filing your copyrights on a regular schedule. Filing your copyrights every two months at a minimum is a good rule to follow, or immediately after you just finished a series of artwork.

KEEPING TRACK OF YOUR COPYRIGHTS

Keep track of when your copyrights have been filed by using a spreadsheet. We have a spreadsheet listing every single one of Drew's paintings and illustrations dating back to the late

1990's. I use it to keep track of what has been filed and what has not yet been filed.

The two main benefits of this spreadsheet:

1. It will be a reminder of what artworks you haven't yet copyrighted (be sure to add each new artwork to the spreadsheet when the artwork is created)
2. In the event of an infringement, you can refer to the spreadsheet and look up the name of the artwork and the date you registered the copyright. This information will be used in your cease & desist letter to the infringer, as well as help you with your legal battle.

Use the following example as a guide to create your own spreadsheet:

Year Created	IMAGE Name	Publish Date	Series or Group	Date © FILED	Date (c) Registration Was received	Registration Date	U.S. (c) Registration Number
2015	Angels & Skulls		Funky Posters Series	8/31/2015	1/14/2016	8/31/2015	V1-625-923
2015	Flying Fish		Funky Posters Group	8/31/2015	1/14/2016	8/31/2015	V1-625-923
2015	Road Less Traveled		Funky Posters Group	8/31/2015	1/14/2016	8/31/2015	V1-625-923
2016	Sacred Waves		N/A	11/15/2016	3/15/2017	10/15/2016	V1-785-015
2016	Sunset Surfing		N/A	11/15/2016	4/15/2017	10/15/2016	V1-785-991
2017	Sitting Mermaid		N/A	Not Yet			
2017	Baja Bad		N/A	Not Yet			

WHEN YOUR WORK IS STOLEN: CEASE & DESIST

What should you do when someone steals your artwork and is selling it as their own?

It depends on the extent of the infringement. If a large company has stolen your work and is distributing it in large quantities, immediately contact an attorney. This could be a payday for you, especially if you filed for copyrights previously.

In 2006 artist Robb Havassy discovered that the giant clothing company, Abercrombie and Fitch, copied art from one of his surfboard paintings and reproduced it onto hundreds of surfboards to use as displays in their stores. They did this without his permission, and what I found to be most disturbing was they even printed the artist's signature on every board! Havassy filed a lawsuit. It took two and a half years for resolution, and though the details were not made public, Havassy received a settlement in an undisclosed sum.

If you never filed copyrights for the images that are being infringed upon, a lawsuit can get expensive, because even if you win, you'll still be responsible for attorney's fees. But, don't let that stop you from taking action to get the infringer to cease and desist use of the stolen art.

If the infringer is an individual, or a small company, you may want to call or write them yourself, rather then involve an attorney. Let the goal be to bring it to their attention and work it out, either by having them cease sales or sign a licensing deal and pay you for it.

A few years ago someone stole Drew's surfboard paintings and resold them in a virtual reality game. We were able to get the infringer on the phone and confront him on the theft. He didn't want us to sue him and asked if we could work it out. We agreed to a $2,500 license fee to Drew, after the fact. We then worked out an ongoing license for future sales. It ended well.

Sometimes another artist will steal your art and sell it to a company, pretending that they designed it. The company often has no idea it is stolen art. This has happened to us a few times. The first was when we had a booth at Surf Expo in 2002. The Hot Girls clothing company who also had a booth was selling Drew's art on one of their t-shirts, the same art we were selling out of our booth! I couldn't believe my eyes. When I confronted the owner about the art, he said a Brazilian artist sold it to him. He didn't believe me at first that it was Drew Brophy's art. It was an exact copy of Drew's iconic *Pure Joy* image. Immediately, I called our attorney and had a cease and desist letter sent. The company agreed to stop selling the tees and they destroyed the screens and all samples they had made.

Another time a concert promoter was using Drew's very popular image *Sunrise* on one of their posters. I got them on the phone and told them that it was Drew's art and they can't use it without permission. They said they had hired an artist in Costa Rica to design the poster and paid her well for it. They didn't know that it was stolen art. They agreed to pay to continue using the artwork and we ended the situation very amicably.

It's too bad for the company when they trust the designers they hire, only to find out later through a lawsuit that the designer infringed on anther artist's work. Many companies will protect themselves by having their artists sign an agreement that says the artwork they are submitting is their own and does not infringe on the rights of anyone else. The language usually states that should there be an infringement lawsuit, the artist is responsible for legal fees, not the company. This is something all artists should be very careful with; not to copy or infringe on another artist's work.

For larger companies, I'll have my attorney send a cease and desist for me. It typically costs about $500. It's worth it, because when the infringing company receives a letter from an attorney, they know you mean business and will take it seriously.

For smaller companies, sometimes I'll draft up my own cease and desist letter. I like to work things out with people when I can. If all I want is for the infringement to stop, then a letter and a phone call will do.

Below is a sample letter I use as a cease and desist.

SAMPLE CEASE & DESIST LETTER

Dear (Insert infringing Artist or company contact name here):

I've become aware that you have made an unauthorized use of my copyrighted Work (herein referred to as Work) entitled _____. Please be aware that I have reserved all rights in the Work, which was first published on _____.

(If you have filed a copyright, include "I have registered copyright for the Work on _____").

Your work (or product) entitled _____ is essentially identical to my copyrighted Work. As you neither asked for nor received permission to use the Work, I believe you have willfully infringed my rights and could be liable for statutory damages.

I demand that you immediately cease the use and distribution of all infringing works derived from the Work, and all copies, including electronic copies, of the same, and that you deliver to me all unused, undistributed copies or destroy such copies immediately and that you desist from this or any other infringement of my rights in the future.

Please respond by email with your agreement to cease and desist.

If you do not comply within 10 business days of the date of this notice, I shall take further action against you in the Federal district court.

Sincerely,

Artist Name Here

Address

Email

Phone

ONLINE INFRINGEMENT

There are people out there who will steal your images and sell them without your permission through third party websites. If this happens to you, don't despair. A DMCA take down notice will stop most infringers. DMCA stands for "The Digital Millennium Copyright Act" and was enacted to protect intellectual property owners from online infringement.

We regularly check on Amazon.com for Drew Brophy knock offs. It's amazing that all I have to do is a search of

"Drew Brophy" and the knock offs will actually have his name in the description! I have shut down many people selling Drew's stolen art printed on t-shirts and cell phone covers.

If you find your work has been stolen and is being sold on eBay, Etsy.com, Amazon, or any other third party site, you'll need to file a DMCA take down notice.

It's easier than it sounds. All you have to do is go to the site and make a claim that someone infringed on your copyrights. They will put a stop to the infringer, and often will cancel their account.

Follow these steps:

1. Take screen shots of the infringement so you can keep a record of it
2. Submit a DMCA takedown notice, either through the website or by letter.

Check the website where the infringing artwork is being displayed and see if they have a form that you can fill out to report copyright infringement. Many sites do, such as Etsy and Amazon. If so, complete their form and follow their instructions.

If the website does not have a form to fill out, then you'll have to send a DMCA Take Down Letter to the hosting company of the website. Some websites are self-hosting, like Facebook. In that case, you would send the letter directly to the website. Other websites are not self-hosting, and so you will have to find out who hosts the website. To do this, you can go to a website such as www.domainsigma.com and do a search to find out who the hosting company is.

Below is a sample letter you can use as a guide. Be sure to include all of your contact information and the information shown in the letter, and send it signed, either with a wet signature or digital signature, as these items are required.

Sample DMCA Take Down Letter:

To Whom it May Concern,

My name is _____ , owner of _____ (company Name here). A website that your company hosts is infringing on copyrights that are owned by me.

I am the copyright owner of the artwork being infringed at this URL: _____.

A screenshot of the artwork being infringed is attached.

This letter is official notification under Section 512 (c) of the Digital Millennium Copyright Act ("DMCA"), and I am asking for the removal of the aforementioned infringing material from your servers.

I am asking that you immediately notify the infringer of this notice and inform them of their duty to remove the infringing material immediately, and notify them to cease any further posting of infringing material to your server in the future.

Please also be advised that law requires you, as a service provider, to quickly remove or disable access to the infringing materials upon receiving this notice. Noncompliance may result in a loss of immunity for liability under the DMCA.

I have good faith belief that use of the image is not authorized by me, the copyright holder, and that my rights are being infringed. Under penalty of perjury I certify that the information contained in the notification is both true and accurate, and I have the authority to act on behalf of the owner of the copyright(s) involved.

Please send me a response to this notice indicating the actions you have taken to resolve this matter.

Thank you for your assistance. Sincerely,

ARTIST NAME

Address

City, State Zip

Phone

E-mail

Keep in mind, laws and their details change often. I am not an attorney, and the information in this section is not meant to give you legal advice. I'm simply sharing what has worked for me. For legal assistance, please contact an attorney in your region that specializes in working with artists. You can also find more up to date information online on DMCA take down notices, as this is a printed book and will not reflect changes in the law that happen after it's printed.

29

READ THE FINE PRINT

When working with corporate clients, galleries or small businesses, you'll often have to put your agreement in writing. Many times, your client will provide you with the written agreement. In the following sections, I'll address several issues to be aware of.

UNDERSTAND AND AGREE WITH IT BEFORE YOU SIGN

Beware of signing any agreement without reading it or understanding it first. You might get locked into something that you either don't want to be locked into, or you might be giving far more than you intended to.

Never sign an agreement that has inaccurate information. If a written agreement does not reflect that which you verbally agreed to, make sure your client corrects it before you sign it. I don't care how great your relationship is with a client, the only thing that matters when things go wrong, is what's written down. Sometimes the person you had a great relationship with leaves the company, and then all you have is what's in writing. Sometimes the company is bought by a bigger company, and all that they go on is what's in writing. The written agreement trumps relationships every time.

One year we had a deal with Sesame Street to have Drew create surf-related Sesame Street characters. In our meetings with them, we agreed to have Drew create the illustrations and license them for printing on apparel and other merchandise. We verbally agreed to an initial $5,000 advance payment up front and royalties on the back end. But, when they sent the contract to me, it stated that we would be paid $5,000 total. No royalties. I called my contact and said that we needed to correct it. I red-lined the contract and made all the corrections. She kept calling, wanting to know why Drew didn't start on the sketches yet. I told her we needed the contract and advance first, and urged her to hurry and send the corrections. Then she asked me to do the unthinkable; sign the contract that's wrong, and we will correct it later. This is something that you should never, ever do. Especially when dealing with a large company. The only thing that matters is the language in the contract, not what they told you. When they refused to correct the contract, the deal died. We were disappointed, but sometimes you just can't work things out.

BEWARE OF SNEAKY TRANSFER OF RIGHTS LANGUAGE

Beware of sneaky language that can trick you into losing all rights to your artwork. Some companies will ask you to sign an agreement, and hidden in the language is wording that transfers all copyright ownership to them. Sometimes it's referred to as "work for hire" and other times it's phrased as "transfer of all rights" or "copyright transfer" or "complete buyout" or some another indication of all rights transferred from the artist to the client.

A "transfer of rights" is different from a "grant of rights". In a transfer, your client becomes the new owner of the artwork and can do anything they want with it.

A temporary grant of rights is a form of licensing. It's a temporary right for the client to use the art and is usually defined in specifics, such as how long the company can use the image (2 years), and for what usage (t-shirts) and where (the U.S. and its territories).

Once you transfer your copyright ownership, you cannot get it back, even if the company goes out of business. When you no longer own your copyrights, you no longer have permission to use the artwork in any way whatsoever, not even for a portfolio or that coffee table book you plan to print in the future.

Many years ago Drew and I experienced the most blatant example ever of a company trying to trick us into giving Drew's art away for a campaign we didn't agree to.

We got a call from one of the largest beer companies in the United States. They asked Drew to paint a surfboard for a give-away they were doing at a surfing event. We were very excited to work with such a large company. They offered $2,500 for Drew to paint their surfboard. We agreed right away.

Then, I received an email from their legal department with a message "attached is a contract, please sign it so we can cut you a check."

I read the contract, and basically it said that the painting that Drew was doing on the surfboard would be considered a "work for hire," which is code for "transferring all copyrights" to the client.

This "work for hire" language was a red flag. Why would they need to own the copyrights? All Drew was doing was painting a surfboard that they planned to give away at a surfing event, or so they claimed.

We set up a conference call with their marketing guy, someone from their legal department, a person from their events department, and myself and Drew. Drew was on our office land-line phone sitting in his back room office, while I was on the other land-line phone at my desk in the front room office. And the call went like this:

Me: "Why do you want to own the artwork? All you're doing is giving the painting away to a winner."

Them: "Oh, we also plan to duplicate the art onto fifty surfboards for charity give-aways."

Me: "That's okay, we will agree to that. I'll write up an agreement that allows for fifty duplicate surfboards. No problem."

Them: "Well.... we also want to use it for in-store point of purchase displays and merchandise for a National marketing campaign."

Now we were talking about an entirely different deal. One little surfboard painting versus an entire advertising, marketing and in-store POP campaign. This type of deal is what can earn you in the six figures easily.

Me: "So, that's an entire marketing campaign using the art. We will agree to that, but, the price will go up quite a bit. Licensing art for such a campaign is an entirely different deal than just painting a surfboard."

Them: "We can't pay more. We don't have a budget."

Then we all heard a loud CLICK on the phone. One of them asked "What was that?"

I said "Drew just hung up."

As you probably guessed, this deal did not go through. About six months later, I called the marketing guy and asked how their campaign went. He said it was a disaster; the artist they ended up hiring to do it didn't understand how to create art for what they needed, and so it didn't translate to advertising. This is a common story, and one I hear again and again.

The moral of this story is this: Always read the fine print when presented with a contract or legal agreement. Trust your instincts, and if something doesn't seem right, it probably isn't. Ask a lot of questions. Make sure you understand it completely and agree to it entirely, before signing it.

In the case of the beer company, they told me one thing but they secretly planned to do another. The contract they sent me was all-telling. The red flag was a warning.

Now, you might be wondering, after reading these two stories of lost deals, if you should stick to your guns on keeping your copyrights and being paid properly. If not, you'll lose deals, right? Well, these stories are not the norm. They are cautionary tales. For every deal that goes bad, we have many good ones that run smoothly.

30

PUT IT IN WRITING

"People still think of me as a cartoonist,
but the only thing I lift a pen or pencil for these
days is to sign a contract, a check, or an autograph."
—Walt Disney

There are two mistakes that artists make when it comes to the business end of selling their art:

1. They aren't putting their agreements with clients in writing, and
2. They sign onerous agreements that can harm their career and earning potential

In this chapter, I will address each one of those issues.

Written agreements seem like extra work, and for an artist, just creating the art is time-consuming enough. But written agreements are important. They help to avoid misunderstandings by clarifying each person's responsibility.

Clarifying is necessary to keep a good relationship with your clients and the friends that you do business with. I use written agreements with everyone, friends included.

Not all agreements have to be in a formal document. Writing up your agreement in a friendly email works for most things.

Three compelling reasons to put your agreements in writing are:

1. To ensure that both parties are agreeing to the same thing. Verbal agreement is where misunderstandings and assumptions happen. Written words provide clarity.

   During the process of drawing up the agreement, you will work out details with your client that you otherwise may not consider.

2. To hold each party accountable for what they've agreed to. Over time, you'll forget exactly what you've agreed to. A written agreement will refresh your memory.

3. To cover your butt. This comes in handy if ever accused of not holding up your end of a deal. You can refer to the agreement and point out that you are. Or you might read it and say, "oh yeah, you're right, I agreed to that!"

When we did a deal with Seven Films to create Drew's instructional DVD titled *Paint Pen Techniques with Drew Brophy*, I asked one of our partners if he wanted to draw up the contract on his end. He said "We don't need a contract. We're good friends." To which I replied "Yes, and if we want to remain friends, we'll need a contract!"

It's a good thing I insisted, because we later discovered inconsistencies in our thinking. I drew up the contract myself, thanks to a very good template that I found online. I made changes to it and outlined the various points that we had all agreed to in our meetings.

When I presented the contract to our partners for review, they shook their heads no. "What?" I asked, confused. They pointed out a few items that they hadn't agreed to. I had misunderstood certain details from our conversations. We discussed it then and there, came to an understanding, and I revised the contract accordingly.

Had we not had a written contract, and that issue came up later, we would have been on opposite ends, arguing about it, and it could have been a problem, which probably would have ended up in losing the friendship as well as the business deal.

For artists, it's especially important to have a written agreement for the following situations:

- Licensing your artwork for products or advertising campaigns
- Consignment of your work through a gallery, charity or retail store
- An event where the artist is hired to attend/perform at
- Any form of partnership where there is a royalty or shared profit
- Representation by an agent

- Animation of your art or use of it in movie or TV productions
- Any partnership of any kind

For the larger deals, I recommend finding an attorney that specializes in the art business. Don't go to a general attorney, as they won't be knowledgeable in the art world. Don't hesitate to pay an attorney to help you with the big stuff; consider it an investment in your business. The smartest business minds know that you have to pay professionals, such as attorneys, to help your business remain healthy and to grow.

You don't have to hire an attorney for everything. For the simpler, smaller deals, you can find licensing and consignment agreement templates online. There are many contracts which you can download and adjust according to your own situation. I also offer many templates that you can access on my website at www.mariabrophy.com.

The good news is that dealing with contracts gets easier and easier. Once you have your templates, you can reuse them over and over again, making minor adjustments to fit each deal.

WHEN A SIMPLE AGREEMENT WILL WORK (INSTEAD OF A FORMAL CONTRACT)

I have witnessed many situations where two people had a verbal agreement and all was going well, until one person thought one thing and the other thought something else. They believed they agreed to the same thing, but they didn't. And there wasn't a paper trail to refer back to.

Not everything needs to be in a formal contract. For most of your deals, an understanding written in an email or proposal will be enough.

When you send your client an offer by email, and they send you an installment payment or an email agreeing with you, it is a signal of their acceptance of your offer.

A simple agreement by email or written proposal can be used for the following situations:

- Commissioned artwork
- Small mural project
- A simple illustration or photography or graphic arts project
- Order for reproduced artwork
- A one-time use license of your work where there is a flat fee payment
- Any simple, uncomplicated agreement between you and your client

The exception to the above list would be if there is a very large sum of money involved and complicated details or if you have much to lose if the other party doesn't hold up their end of the deal. If you aren't sure, get advice from an attorney.

A simple email agreement can be written in the body of the email, or you could take it a professional notch further and write it up in a separate document that is attached in your email.

The agreement can either be in the form of a proposal for the client to accept, or a write up of what you and your client already agreed to. All details should be spelled out, including the basics, such as:

- Scope of work (Description or Deliverables)
- Size, medium and materials used
- Price and payment schedule, including installment payment requirement
- Who the payment will be made out to or how it will be made
- What rights are included / what is not included
- A "kill fee" if applicable (i.e. kill fee of 75% is due in full within five business days, should client cancel the project.)
- Projected timeline
- Copyright ownership
- Expectations of either party, if applicable
- Next steps (i.e. "the next step is for you to show acceptance of this proposal by sending the installment payment")

Not every project requires a contract, but every project requires a written account of what each party is responsible for, and when.

This becomes easy after you write up a few. You can save your document as a template and use the same template again and again, just change the details each time.

WHAT IF A CLIENT WON'T SIGN AN AGREEMENT

Sometimes you'll have a client who doesn't want to sign a contract. They will say cute things like "I believe in the handshake deal" and "I run my business on trust." That works, if you're running a lemonade stand! But if you are going into a deal where a signed, written agreement is absolutely necessary, you'll have to convince them that a contract is important not just for you, but for them, too.

Usually, when a client is afraid to sign a contract, it means one of two things; they are either inexperienced in this type of deal and it makes them nervous, or they are in the habit of not taking care of business in this manner. It's up to you to gently guide them to sign it.

We installed Drew's art in a gallery in Newport Beach, CA. I had emailed the owner a consignment agreement weeks before, but he never signed it. So when we went to install the art, I brought him a printed agreement and asked him to sign it. He didn't want to; he told me that none of the artists in his gallery had a consignment agreement. I explained to him that it's important to us, as we need a paper trail should there be a natural disaster or bankruptcy. I told him that the agreement gives him permission to give discounts to his collectors, and it details the pricing. It's in his best interest to have the agreement. I also explained that we never do consignments without an agreement. He smiled, grabbed a pen and signed it.

AGREEMENTS THAT CAN HARM YOU

When a client or agent provides an agreement to you, be sure that you understand fully what you are agreeing to before signing it.

I'm always surprised when I hear that someone signed a contract without even reading or understanding it. How do you know what you're agreeing to without reading it? And if you don't know what you are agreeing to, how can you hold up your end of the agreement?

Please, never sign a contract that you don't fully understand.

One of my artist clients signed a five-year contract with a manufacturing company to license her artwork. They paid her no money up front, and the contract stated that they got the exclusive rights to all of her artwork and that she couldn't sell the art to anyone else. They verbally promised her big dollars, but in the two years after they signed the agreement, they had paid her $0. She couldn't sell her work to anyone else, either. She was stuck in a terrible contract for five years, one that prevented her from making any money from her art. Luckily, we got her out of that contact but it took a lot of work and it was highly stressful for her. She had lost two years of income because of it.

I'm not telling you this to scare you out of signing contracts. I want to encourage you to take great care with your business and your copyrights and your name and everything else that is near and dear to your existence as an artist.

EVERY CONTRACT IS NEGOTIABLE

When you are presented with a contract and it contains language that you don't agree with, don't hesitate to ask your client to make changes to it. Every contract is negotiable.

When working with a licensee, client or agent, you'll often be presented with a contract that they use for all artists. The thing is, all artists are different; their business models are different, their art is different, their brand is different. What works for one artist will not work for another. There is no such thing as "one size fits all" with contracts.

It's not only okay to ask for changes to a contract, it's often expected. Most of your clients will want you to feel good about what you're signing. They want you to be happy. Most of them are not trying to harm you.

If you don't understand something that is in a contract, call your client and ask them to explain it to you. And if you don't agree with their explanation, ask them to change it to something you will agree with.

Below are just a few examples of bad contract language I've seen in my career, and how I remedy it:

- A long term or no end date to the contract, meaning they have you locked in forever – this can harm your future as a career artist. Ask them to change it to a shorter term, such as 2 or 3 years.
- "Work for Hire" or "buy out" or "transfer of rights" language – where the client is taking ownership of your copyrights. Tell them you don't do work for hire, but

you will happily grant temporary rights. Change the contract to reflect licensing rather than buy-out.

- Non-compete language – this means they won't allow you to work with other companies in their industry for a period of time, thus harming your future ability to earn a living. Tell them you can't agree to this, but if they are concerned about a specific competitor, you might agree to not selling to that one competitor for a short period of time.

- First rights of refusal – this means you are obligated to show them all new work first, before showing or selling to another client. Never agree to this without great financial compensation attached. Instead, tell them it would interfere with your business model, but that you are happy to show them any work that you feel they will be interested in; you just don't want to be obligated to do so in a contract.

I could list about 100 more things to add to this, but that is another book for me to write. The items listed are some of the red flags that pop up frequently.

When there is language that I don't agree with or that conflicts with our business model, I ask the client to change it. Many times, the client doesn't even know why the language is in their contract. Sometimes they are using an old contract or one they found off of the internet. Sometimes they hired legal counsel that has no understanding of how artists work. In other words, it's not usually malicious or that they are trying to take advantage of you. It's that they just don't know. It's up to you to educate them on how you work and what you are willing to agree to.

Most of the time, a client will make the changes I ask for. Sometimes we have to compromise. If they don't want to make the changes I requested, I take the time to find out why. Usually it's because they are worried about something that I was unaware of, and once I find out what that is, I can come up with a creative way to create language that alleviates their concerns while not giving up on what's important to me.

Most artists are afraid to have conversations with their clients when it comes to contracts. Don't fear asking questions and having these discussions! It's crucial to have friendly conversations at the beginning stages of a relationship, to make sure you are all on the same page. The contract phase brings up a lot of topics that you otherwise wouldn't have talked about. It's a tool to help you and your client communicate on the nitty gritty details.

To recap, there are three rules to follow when it comes to written agreements:

1. Always have an agreement with a client in writing, either in a formal contract, or an informal email or document that details what you and your client are agreeing to.

2. Never sign anything that you don't fully agree to or don't understand. Every contract is negotiable. You can make changes to every contract presented to you, to fit your needs.

3. Make it clear to your clients and collectors that you retain ownership to the copyrights of your artwork. This can be written on your invoices, website, written agreements, and any other place your work is displayed.

Legal disclaimer: Please note that I am not an attorney, and that any information in this book should not be construed as legal advice. I am simply sharing my own personal opinions and business practices, based on my experience in the business of art. For legal advice, consult an artist's attorney in your region.

31

BUSINESS SYSTEMS

"We are what we repeatedly do.
Excellence, then, is not an act, but a habit."
—Aristotle

Have you ever missed a sale because you failed to follow up with a potential buyer? It happened to me once, and I still regret it years later.

An interested buyer had walked into our studio. He was a tall, distinguished man. He was ready to buy, but first needed his wife's agreement. Before he left, I got his name and number and said I would follow up with him the next day.

But that piece of paper got lost on my desk. I got busy and assumed he'd call me. I never called him and I never heard from him again. I found out later that he ended up buying a large art piece from another local artist.

It was my lack of organization and follow up that lost the sale. I'm still kicking myself over that. But since then, I implemented a system of following up on hot prospects, and I will never lose a sale again.

SYSTEMS SAVE TIME

I have to admit, I'm not as efficient as I would like to be. I get so easily distracted by so many things. It seems like my to-do list is so long that I'll never get caught up. If you're like me, you probably wish you had more time in the day to do everything you want to do.

In this business of art, there are so many little things that must be done. Some of these little things are very important (but no fun) like filing copyrights, bookkeeping or making follow up calls to potential clients. We can get more done in less time if we implement systems for ourselves.

MOST EVERYTHING WE DO IS A HABIT OR SYSTEM

From the moment we wake up to the time we go to sleep, our actions are run by our habits and systems.

Many habits were programmed into us at a very young age, such as brushing our teeth and getting dressed. Some we trained ourselves to do when we got older, like writing a daily to-do list or meditating in the morning.

Everything we do is either handled in a conscious way (with a system), or in a half-hazard way (no system). With a system, we can decide in advance how we want to respond to recurring events. Creating a system is very much like creating a good habit, like brushing your teeth every day.

With a system in place, we can make the best possible decisions and take the best actions, consistently. Without a system, we are floating like a leaf in the wind, reacting to things rather than responding. Without a system, we are not automatically directing our energy to a pre-planned intention. Tasks take longer and we waste time re-inventing the wheel. And we are working twice as hard!

However, once we put a system in place, we no longer have to use extra time to think about how we will do something, because it becomes automatic. Setting up a system takes a little time at first, but it saves hours of time later. And that's what we all want, right? More Time!

EMAIL INQUIRY SYSTEM

Many of the inquiries for Drew's artwork ask the same questions over and over, such as: "How much does it cost to get a commissioned painting?" and "Can Drew paint my surfboard?"

For years, I wrote responses to each inquiry as they came. This was a time waster, because essentially I was writing the same thing again and again. Each time I got an email, I had to use time and brain power to write the responses.

Finally, it dawned on me that I could set up a system to save time. I now have canned responses to the recurring questions, titled "Surfboard Painting Inquiry" and "Commissioned Painting Inquiry." I store these responses in my Google Drive so I can copy and paste the response into an email reply, add a little personalization to it, and hit "send."

HOT FOLLOW UPS FOLDER

After sending a price quote or response to an email inquiry, I move the email into a folder titled "Hot Follow Ups." Two times a week I go into that folder and review it, so that I can be reminded of who I should call or email to follow up with.

The beauty of using the "Hot Follow Ups" folder is the result I see in revenue; we are getting more painting sales because of the simple act of remembering (following the system) to follow up with everyone in that folder.

CREATIVE SYSTEM

When Drew is about to begin a new painting series, he has a system that ensures that the series will be executed efficiently and in a well thought out manner:

- First, he decides the theme of the series.
- He envisions the results he wants from it; such as what impact he wants the art to make on people, and how much $ he plans to earn from the sales of the art.
- He draws rough ideas on paper and determines how many pieces and what size each one will be. He envisions how the pieces will look in an exhibit or the venue where it will be.

- Next, he clears space in the back room of the studio where he paints. He sweeps the floor and clears out all non-essentials to make room to paint all the new blank canvas.
- Then, he goes to San Clemente Art Supply store and buys all of the art supplies.
- Lastly, when everything is in order, he begins painting with a clear vision, a clean room and everything he needs right at his fingertips.

BUSINESS SYSTEMS THAT WILL SAVE TIME

Here is a short list of areas where you can create habits and systems for efficiency, consistency and results:

- Plan your day first thing each morning by writing your most important goals and intentions.
- Use software or spreadsheets that manages your inventory and keep track of work that you have on hand or have sold.
- Systemize the collecting of names for your email list.
- File copyrights every two months or when you finish a series of work.

You can also create a system...

- For when an artwork is created (add to your master copyright spreadsheet, add to your website for sale, include in your next newsletter)

- For when an artwork is sold (capture the buyer's information, ship it, add to your master artwork spreadsheet, follow up with buyer a week later with a thank you, etc.)
- To follow up after sales (to connect with buyers, galleries, agencies or licensees, etc.)
- To nourish your network (how you will keep in touch with past buyers and associates)

HOW TO IMPLEMENT YOUR SYSTEMS

Where are there redundancies in your daily, weekly and monthly activities? Choose just one area to begin with. Below are two examples.

If you sell illustrations to corporate clients, you would create a system of "New Client Follow Up." As an example, your system could look like this:

- Email your new prospect to set up a discovery phone call
- Add them to your master list of prospects.
- Write up a proposal and send it to the client.
- Within 24 hours, follow up by email to confirm they received the proposal.
- If they do not respond with a yes or a no, follow up in 72 hours with a phone call. Ask them for a yes or a no.
- If they don't accept your proposal, ask why. Find out if there is a way to provide them with a proposal they will accept.

- If they still don't accept your proposal, thank them for your time. Then put a reminder on your calendar to follow up in three months and ask "how did your project go?" and ask if they have any other projects for you.

If you sell paintings, you would create a system of "When a Piece of Art is Created." As an example, your system could look like this:

- Capture a high resolution photo of it
- Sign and name the art piece
- Add the piece to your Master Artwork Inventory list (software or spreadsheet)
- Add the piece to your Master Copyright spreadsheet
- Write up a compelling description about it
- Post it to your online store for sale or send to your gallery
- Send out an email newsletter announcement
- Post on social media with a link to online store or a way to purchase
- File for copyright(s)
- Sell it

Write up your steps and keep it handy to remind yourself of the system you decided to implement. Then take the action required to ensure that you consistently use the system, for example, by putting reminders on your calendar.

Think of one system that you can implement today, to make an area of your business run more efficiently, with less time and effort.

32

PUT YOUR NAME ON IT

*"Every thought you produce, anything you say,
any action you do, it bears your signature."*
—Thich Nhat Hanh

Make sure that your name, signature or logo is printed or signed on everything your art is displayed on. This includes original pieces, digital artwork and reproductions on products.

Your signature announces who the artist is and at the same time promotes your work further. If you can't put your name on the front of a piece for aesthetic reasons, then create a symbol that can be printed or painted in a subtle way in every art piece. Or, sign your name to the back.

For licensed products, your name and/or signature should be on every piece as well as the packaging and all advertising.

It does your future no good to create a piece of art and then have no one know who did it. For artists who are creating high volume of work, or are being copied often, or are creating influential works, your name authenticates the artwork. It's an indication that it is an official art piece of yours, rather than a knock off.

I remember being in Hawaii one year and seeing a beautiful piece of artwork on a poster in a surf shop. I looked for the artist's name or signature, but nowhere on that amazing piece of artwork was any indication of who the artist was. To this day, I wonder why the artist didn't insist that their name be clearly printed on that poster. They missed out on a great opportunity to market their work in an easy way.

In the summer of 2016, we received a call from Pearl Jam's front man, Eddie Vedder's, merchandise manager. Eddie was putting on a new music festival called The 'Ohana Fest and hand-picked Drew to create the poster artwork for the event.

We were so happy because we love Eddie Vedder and he is by far the biggest music star we have ever worked with. We came to an agreement on price, they paid their installment payment, and Drew went to work on the art.

A month later, when the posters for the 'Ohana Fest were plastered all over town with Drew's illustration on them, we felt proud! People loved the posters so much that many of them "disappeared" from store windows. The best thing of all was that Drew's signature and logo was clearly printed on the posters.

Often, if you don't ask to have your name clearly printed on an item, the client won't do it. It's up to *you* to make sure this happens.

In your earlier conversations with your client, say "I will want to make sure my name or signature is clearly legible on the items being printed." Make it crystal clear in the beginning what you expect.

If you are licensing your work, a good license agreement will include the requirement that your signature or logo or copyright notice be printed legibly on the items.

If you are doing a small or one-off project where a licensing agreement is not being used, make it clear verbally and in writing that you require this.

And then, follow up before they go to print with the work, and ask to see a sample. They can email you a mock-up of what they plan on printing. You want to see it before it goes to print to ensure that they placed your name properly and clearly as promised. Sometimes they forget to do this, and it's up to you to remind them.

SCRIPT: When a client is using your art to be printed or reproduced on items, include this statement in your agreement or email correspondence:

"It is required that my _____ (Fill in your requirement – signature, name, logo and/or copyright notice "Artwork (c) Mary Artist") is clearly and legibly printed on the artwork. Please send me a sample of what you plan to print prior to printing it for my approval."

If your client doesn't follow through on including your signature or name, make them correct the error. Usually it's an oversight on their end, and it's up to you to make sure they correct it.

33

TESTIMONIALS

If your business model includes being commissioned to create work of any kind, testimonials from past clients will help you gain new clients.

When investing money into art, buyers want to be sure the person they are commissioning is legit. Testimonials from real people help to give a new buyer confidence in your abilities to give them what they want.

A good testimonial comes from the heart of your client and captures, in their own words, the value that you brought to them. On my website, www.mariabrophy.com, I posted a page of testimonials from artists and small business owners that I have helped in the past. I asked permission to use their full name, because I want new readers to know that I am posting real words from real people.

Here's an example of a testimonial on my site that captures what I do best, comes from the heart of my client and will help new clients decide if I can help them or not:

"I haven't had a conversation with someone this knowledgeable in my whole life! A lot of people tell me that I should sell my work, but you are the first person who has been able to tell me HOW, in a viable way." –Joe Mahoney

On Drew's website, www.drewbrophy.com, we posted a page of testimonials from his corporate clients. Here's an example of a testimonial we received from our contact at the marketing company that hired us to do a project for Verizon:

"We worked with Drew to transform our Verizon FiOS VW Bus into a work of art during the US Open of Surf. It was effortless working with Drew and Maria. They had very little time to plan and design, yet the final result was more than what we could have asked for."

You'll notice one thing about all of the testimonials on both mine and Drew's websites: we use the client's full name. This gives authenticity to the testimonial. Otherwise, a reader may not be convinced that the testimonial is real.

HOW TO GET TESTIMONIALS

The most effective testimonials are those that are short, give specific details and are straight from the client's heart. Some people are afraid to ask for a testimonial from a client. Don't be afraid. If your client enjoyed the work you did for them, they will be happy to allow you to use their words as a testimonial.

And, there's an easy way to ask your client that doesn't require any work from them at all. The best way to get an authentic, from-the-heart testimonial, is to:

1. call your client on the phone and ask them the right questions (see scripts below)
2. write down what they say, and
3. use what they said (with their permission) as a testimonial.

Script of questions to get your client to speak from the heart:

"I want to follow up and ask a few questions. Were you pleased with the work I did for you?"

Then, ask, "What did you like best about the work I did for you?"

These questions are meant to get the client to speak in specifics. Listen and write notes as they talk. After you were able to get them to share their feelings about working with you, say:

"I would like to use some of what you said as a testimonial. I'll write it up and email it to you for your permission. Is that okay?"

Most people will say yes. And they will appreciate that you did all the work for them! I haven't had anyone tell me no yet.

Next, write up a short, concise testimonial using their own words, email it to them and ask permission to use it on your portfolio and website, along with their full name (and company name, if applicable).

This is the best way to get a testimonial, for two reasons:

1. You are doing all the work so you make it easy for your client; and
2. By asking them questions, without first telling them WHY you're asking, you get to the heart of how they felt when working with you. This gets the best testimonials of all!

Make it a habit to collect testimonials from your clients every time you finish a project. Post them on your website on a page titled "testimonials" or "praise" or "happy customers." You can also pull the best ones and use them in sales brochures and marketing materials.

34

CREATE WITHOUT FEAR - YOUR BIG IDEA

*"Do whatever brings you to life, then. Follow your own
fascinations, obsessions, and compulsions. Trust them.
Create whatever causes a revolution in your heart."*
—Elizabeth Gilbert, in Big Magic:
Creative Living Beyond Fear

Even the most talented among us have doubts. The difference between those making things happen and those who aren't is this: the people who make things happen take action on their ideas in spite of fears, doubts and critics.

In January of 2014 an artist asked, "Will you look at my painting and tell me if I should keep painting or just end it with this one."

Her self doubt and fear was evident, and I didn't want to add to it. When I get emails like this, I know that my response will either encourage or discourage. Since I'm not God, I have no idea what this artist is meant to be doing, and so I wanted to guide her to guide herself, based on her own instinct.

But, being able to help someone understand that their own inner guidance is the best guidance can be difficult. So I decided to simplify it. I wrote back, "It doesn't matter what I think. Keep painting if it brings you joy!"

I didn't hear back from her until two years later, when she wrote, "You probably don't remember me, but, I took your advice. I have since completed 61 paintings and have just been invited by a gallery for a solo exhibition. Thank you."

Sometimes we think that we need permission from someone to move forward. It's as though we don't trust ourselves.

Artists will pay me a consulting fee just to hear me say, "It's okay, do what you dream of doing." Upon hearing those words, they are energized, as if my opinion matters.

But you don't need anyone's permission and it doesn't matter what anyone thinks of your art or your ideas. The only thing that matters is you. Keep doing what brings you joy, and others will eventually feel the joy of it, too.

THE HANDS PROJECT

One artist who has given birth to a big idea is Joan Chamberlain. She aspires to become known for drawing hands. She has committed to carrying out a vision that she calls "The Hands Project".

In The Hands Project, Joan's drawings capture the beauty of the busy hands of gifted chefs.

Joan is a cook and foodie, and she explains on her website why drawing chef's hands is important to her:

"I am keenly aware of the thousands of manipulations that a chef's hands undertake in the course of their work. I am fascinated with the seemingly effortless choreography of hand movement from one task to another in the kitchen. I have a dream of building a collection of drawings showcasing the hands of chefs."

The Hands Project is a great example of a unique idea that involves a lot of time and patience to execute. In the end, The Hands Project will generate an impact on the way people view a chef's work.

Ten years from now, when the world thinks of hands, they will think of Joan Chamberlain.

Have the courage to do what you believe in. Create in a way that you are driven to create. If you're inspired by an idea, forge ahead and do it. Don't worry about what others think of it.

Your ideas will take on a life of their own as you lean into it. Take that first step, and the rest will fall into place.

TEN THOUSAND BUDDHAS

Just yesterday I was walking around the Abbott Kinney area of Venice Beach, California, and I spotted one of the Buddha murals of artist Amanda Giacomini.

I was excited to run into this mural, as I had previously read about the Ten Thousand Buddhas project and have been drawn to it.

Amanda Giacomini is on an artistic journey to create Ten Thousand Buddhas. She paints her Buddhas on large scale public murals, oil paintings, screen prints and antique wooden Tibetan prayer wheels.

Giacomini gave birth to this grandiose idea and acted on it. She didn't need permission from anyone. She just started painting Buddhas. You can now see her Buddha walls all over the U.S. and her Buddha paintings and prints are collected worldwide.

Now, when I think of Buddhas, I think of Giacomini's beautiful artwork. That's the power of intention, commitment and consistency.

YOUR BIG IDEA

When you decide to make an impact with your work, you give birth to it the moment you take the first action.

Over time, your ideas will grow and take on a life of their own. Word gets out, and the next thing you know, people want to help make your dream happen. The entire Universe conspires to bring your vision to life.

Commitment, consistency and deliberate action is what grows your project from the seed of an idea to one that makes an impact on the world. But you have to take that first step. The rest will fall into place.

Many people hesitate to be the first to do something huge. They worry about it not being important, or they worry that no one will understand what they're doing. They worry about the details, and obsess over how it will come to life.

Don't worry about critics, they will always be there annoying us. Don't concern yourself with the details. Amanda Giacomini didn't worry about where she was going to find the walls to paint ten thousand Buddhas. She started with the first one.

When you set the intention and take action on your ideas, the walls will come. The people will show up. The opportunities will present themselves. Trust enough to take that first step. Commit to doing what you believe in. And then, the rest of the world will come around.

What big idea will you commit to? What are you driven to create to make an impact? Lean into it, take the first step, and watch it fall into place.

Recommended Reading

Handbook: Pricing and Ethical Guidelines by The Graphic Artist's Guild

Art-Write: The Writing Guide for Visual Artists by Vicki Krohn Amerose

I'd Rather be in the Studio by Alyson Stanfield

Legal Guide for the Visual Artist by Tad Crawford

How to Sell your Art Online: Live a Successful Creative Life on Your own Terms by Cory Huff

How to Survive and Prosper as an Artist by Caroll Michels

Fine Art Tips by Lori McNee

Big Magic: Creative Living Beyond Fear by Elizabeth Gilbert

How to Profit from the Art Print Market 2nd Edition: Creating Cash Flow from Original Art by Barney Davey

The Success Principles: How to get From Where You Are to Where You Want to Be by Jack Canfield and Janet Switzer

Titles by Maria Brophy:

How to Understand Art Licensing Agreements by Maria Brophy and Tara Reed

Living the Dream by Maria Brophy

How to Make Money Painting at Live Events by Maria Brophy

How to Draw with Drew Brophy by Drew Brophy and Maria Brophy

Biography

Maria Brophy has been an art agent to her husband Drew Brophy since 2001, and a business consultant to creative entrepreneurs since 2009. In her former life, Maria worked in the corporate world for two agonizing decades before she escaped the 9 to 5 grind. Since then, she's deliberately designed her life as a non-stop adventure, traveling extensively with her husband and two kids while surfing and backpacking some of the most magical places in the world. She's also authored several books on business and produced a television show called The Paint Shop with Drew Brophy. Now she works one-on-one with artists and spiritual entrepreneurs, helping them to learn powerful business strategies that will enable them to realize their own dream lifestyles.

Maria's primary wish is to guide entrepreneurs to easily carry out their own mission of healing and creativity. She believes that the term "starving artist" will become a silly thing of the past. She's doing her part to put that paradigm to rest for good.

Visit www.mariabrophy.com and sign up for the free email series, *11 weeks of business strategies that you can put into action right away.* And please email your questions and success stories, to consulting@mariabrophy.com.

42851922R00195